THE POSSE LAY IN WAIT . . .

"Watch for 'em sneakin' up on us," the sheriff warned. "They's three of 'em, and most likely they'll come at us three ways."

A light patter caught Vic's ear, like the running of many small children over a heavy carpet, and then the shadows rushed into view: the black stallion and Bart, the wolf-dog, fleeting in front. Surprise was complete.

Even before Vic heard the posse's shots ring out, Satan leaped high. Straight across the pale moon—a winged horse with a buoyant figure upon it. It cleared a five-foot rock and rushed instantly out of view among the boulders.

The fugitive had fired only one shot, and that when the stallion was at the crest of its leap. It found its mark—one man lay dead—shot cleanly through the head.

MAX BRAND

THE SEVENTH MAN

WARNER
PAPERBACK
LIBRARY

A Warner Communications Company

WARNER PAPERBACK LIBRARY EDITION
First Printing: October, 1974

This Warner Paperback Library Edition is published
by arrangement with Dodd, Mead and Company, Inc.

Cover illustration by Carl Hantman

Warner Paperback Library is a division of Warner Books, Inc.,
75 Rockefeller Plaza, New York, N.Y. 10019.

W A Warner Communications Company

Printed in the United States of America

CHAPTER I

Spring

A man under thirty needs neighbors and to stop up the current of his life with a long silence is like obstructing a river—eventually the water either sweeps away the dam or rises over it, and the stronger the dam the more destructive is that final rush to freedom. Vic Gregg was on the danger side of thirty and he lived alone in the mountains all that winter. He wanted to marry Betty Neal, but marriage means money, therefore Vic contracted fifteen hundred dollars' worth of mining for the Duncans, and instead of taking a partner he went after that stake single-handed. He is a very rare man who can turn out that amount of labor in a single season, but Gregg furnished that exception which establishes the rule: he did the assessment work on fourteen claims and almost the fifteenth, yet he paid the price. Week after week his set of drills was wife and child to him, and for conversation he had only the clangor of the four-pound single-jack on the drill heads, with the crashing of the "shots" now and then as periods to the chatter of iron on iron. He kept at it, and in the end he almost finished the allotted work, but for all of it he paid in full.

The acid loneliness ate into him. To be sure, from boyhood he knew the mountain quiet, the still heights and the solemn echoes, but towards the close of the long isolation the end of each day found him oppressed by a weightier sense of burden; in a few days he would begin to talk to himself. From the first the evening pause after supper hurt him most, for a man needs a talk as well as tobacco, and after a time he dreaded these evenings so bitterly that he purposely spent himself every day, so as to pass from supper into sleep at a stride. It needed a long day to burn out his strength thoroughly, so he set his rusted alarm-clock, and before dawn it brought him groaning out of the blankets to cook a hasty breakfast and go slowly up to the tunnel. In short, he wedded himself to his work; he stepped into a routine which took the place of thought, and the change in him was so gradual that he did not see the danger.

A mirror might have shown it to him as he stood this morning at the door of his lean-to for the wind fluttered the shirt around his labor-dried body, and his forehead puckered in a frown, grown habitual. It was a narrow face, with rather close-set eyes and a slanted forehead which gave token of a single-track mind, a single-purposed nature with one hundred and eighty pounds of strong sinews and iron-hard muscle to give it significance. Such was Vic Gregg as he stood at the door waiting for the coffee he had drunk to brush away the cobwebs of sleep, and then he heard the eagle scream.

A great many people have never heard the scream of an eagle. The only voice they connect with the kind of the air is a ludicrously feeble squawk, dim with distance, but in his great moments the eagle has a war-cry like that of the hawk, but harsher, hoarser, ten-fold in volume. This sound cut into the night in the gulch, and Vic Gregg started and glanced about for echoes made the sound stand at his side; then he looked up, and saw two eagles fighting in the light of the morning. He knew what it meant—the beginning of the mating season, and these two battling for a prize. They darted away. They flashed together with reaching talons and gaping beaks, and dropped in a tumult of wings, then soared and clashed once more until one of them folded his wings and dropped bullet-like out of the morning into the night. Close over Gregg's head, the wings flirted out—ten feet from tip to tip—beat down with a great washing sound, and the bird shot across the valley in a level flight.

The conqueror screamed a long insult down the hollow. For a while he balanced, craning his bald head as if he sought applause, then, without visible movement of

6

his wings, sailed away over the peaks. A feather fluttered slowly down past Vic Gregg.

He looked down to it, and rubbed the ache out of the back of his neck. All about him the fresh morning was falling; yonder shone a green-mottled face of granite, and there a red iron blow-out streaked with veins of glittering silicate, and in this corner, still misted with the last delicate shades of night, glimmered rhyolite, lavender-pink. The single-jack dropped from the hand of Gregg, and his frown relaxed.

When he stretched his arms, the cramps of labor un-kinked and let the warm blood flow, swiftly, and in the pleasure of it he closed his eyes and drew a luxurious breath. He stepped from the door with his head high and his heart lighter, and when his hobnailed shoe clinked on the fallen hammer he kicked it spinning from his path. That act brought a smile into his eyes, and he sauntered to the edge of the little plateau and looked down into the wide chasm of the Asper valley.

Blue shadows washed across it, though morning shone around Gregg on the height, and his glance dropped in a two-thousand-foot plunge to a single yellow eye that winked through the darkness, a light in the trapper's cabin. But the dawn was falling swiftly now, and while Gregg lingered the blue grew thin, purple-tinted, and then dark, slender points pricked up, which he knew to be the pines. Last of all, he caught the sheen of grass.

Around him pressed a perfect silence, the quiet of night holding over into the day, yet he cast a glance behind him as he heard a voice. Indeed, he felt that some one approached him, some one for whom he had been waiting, yet it was a sad expectancy, and more like home-sickness than anything he knew.

"Aw, hell," said Vic Gregg, "it's spring."

A deep-throated echo boomed back at him, and the sound went down the gulch, three times repeated.

"Spring," repeated Gregg more softly, as if he feared to rouse that echo, "damned if it ain't!"

He shrugged his shoulders and turned resolutely towards the lean-to, picking up the discarded hammer on the way. By instinct he caught it at exactly the right balance

7

for his strength and arm, and the handle, polished by his grip, played with an oiled, frictionless movement against the callouses of his palm. From the many hours of drilling, fingers crooked, he could only straighten them by a painful effort. A bad hand for cards, he decided gloomily, and still frowning over this he reached the door. There he paused in instant repugnance, for the place was strange to him.

In thought and wish he was even now galloping Grey Molly over the grass along the Asper, and he had to wrench himself into the mood of the patient miner. There lay his blankets, rumpled, brown with dirt, and he shivered at sight of them; the night had been cold. Before he fell asleep, he had flung the magazine into the corner and now the wind rustled its torn, yellowed pages in a whisper that spoke to Gregg of the ten-times repeated stories, tales of adventure, drifts of tobacco smoke in gaming halls, the chant of the croupier behind the wheel, deep voices of men, laughter of pretty girls, tattoo of running horses, shouts which only red-eye can inspire. He sniffed the air; odor of burned bacon and coffee permeated the cabin. He turned to the right and saw his discarded overalls with ragged holes at the knees; he turned to the left and looked into the face of the rusted alarm clock. Its quick, soft ticking sent an ache of weariness through him.

"What's wrong with me," muttered Gregg. Even that voice seemed ghostly loud in the cabin, and he shivered again. "I must be going nutty."

As if to escape from his own thoughts, he stepped out into the sun again, and it was so grateful to him after the chill shadow in the lean-to, that he looked up, smiling, into the sky. A west wind urged a scattered herd of clouds over the peaks, tumbled masses of white which puffed into transparent silver at the edges, and behind, long wraiths of vapor marked the path down which they had traveled. Such an old cow-hand as Vic Gregg could not fail to see the forms of cows and heavy-necked bulls and running calves in that drift of clouds. About this season the boys would be watching the range for signs of screw worms in the cattle, and the bog-riders must have their hands full dragging out cows which had fled into the mud to escape the heel flies. With a new lonesomeness he drew his eyes down to the mountains.

Ordinarily, strange fancies never entered the hard head of Gregg, but to-day it seemed to him that the mountains found a solemn companionship in each other. Out of the horizon, where the snowy forms glimmered in the blue, they marched in loose order down to the valley of the Asper, where some of them halted in place, huge cliffs, and others stumbled out into foothills, but the main range swerved to the east beside the valley, eastward out of his vision, though he knew that they went on to the town of Alder.

Alder was Vic Gregg's Athens and Rome in one, its schoolhouse his Acropolis, and Captain Lorrimer's saloon his Forum. Other people talked of larger cities, but Alder satisfied the imagination of Vic; besides, Grey Molly was even now in the blacksmith's pasture, and Betty Neal was teaching in the school. Following the march of the mountains and the drift of the clouds, he turned towards Alder. The piled water shook the dam, topped it, burst it into fragments, and rushed into freedom; he *must* go to Alder, have a drink, shake hands with a friend, kiss Betty Neal, and come back again. Two days going, two days coming, three days for the frolic; a week would cover it all. And two hours later Vic Gregg had cached his heavier equipment, packed his necessaries on the burro, and was on the way.

By noon he had dropped below the snowline and into the foothills, and with every step his heart grew lighter. Behind him the mountains slid up into the heart of the sky with cold, white winter upon them, but here below it was spring indubitably. There was hardly enough fresh grass to temper the winter brown into shining bronze, but a busy, awakening insect life thronged through the roots. Surer signs than this, the flowers were coming. A slope of buttercups flashed suddenly when the wind struck it and wild morning-glory spotted a stretch of daisies with purple and dainty lavender. To be sure, the blossoms never grew thickly enough to make strong dashes of color, but they tinted and stained the hillsides. He began to

9

cross noisy little watercourses, empty most of the year, but now the melting snow fed them. From eddies and quiet pools the bright watercress streamed out into the currents, and now and then in moist ground under a sheltering bank he found rich patches of violets.

His eyes went happily among these tokens of the glad time of the year, but while he noted them and the bursting buds of the aspen, reddish-brown, his mind was open to all that middle register of calls which the human ear may notice in wild places. Far above his scale were shrilling murmurs of birds and insects, and beneath it ran those ground noises that the rabbit, for instance, understands so well; but between these overtones and undertones he heard the scream of the hawk, spiraling down in huge circles, and the rapid call of a grouse, far off, and the drone of insects about his feet, or darting suddenly upon his brain and away again. He heard these things by the grace of the wind, which sometimes blew them about him in a chorus, and again shut off all except that lonely calling of the grouse, and often whisked away every murmur and left Gregg in the center of a wide hush with only the creak of the pack-saddle and the click of the burro's accurate feet among the rocks.

At such times he gave his full attention to the trail, and he read it as one might turn the pages of a book. He saw how a rabbit had scurried, running hard, for the prints of the hind feet planted far ahead of those on the fore paws. There was reason in her haste, for here the pads of a racing coyote had dug deeply into a bit of soft ground. The sign of both rabbit and coyote veered suddenly, and again the trail told the reason clearly—the big print of a lobo's paw, that gray ghost which haunts the ranges with the wisest brain and the swiftest feet in the West. Vic Gregg grinned with excitement; fifty dollars' bounty if that scalp were his! But the story of the trail called him back with the sign of some small animal which must have traveled very slowly, for in spite of the tiny size of the prints, each was distinct. The man sniffed with instinctive aversion and distrust, for this was the trail of the skunk, and if the last of the seven sleepers was out, it was spring indeed. He raised his cudgel and thwacked the burro joyously.

"Get on, Mame," he cried. "We're overdue in Alder." Mame switched her tail impatiently and canted back a long ear to listen, but she did not increase her pace; for Mame had only one gait, and if Vic occasionally thumped her, it was rather by way of conversation than in any hope of hurrying their journey.

CHAPTER II

Grey Molly

If her soul had been capable of enthusiasm, Mame could have made the trip on schedule time, but she was a burro good for nothing except to carry a pack well nigh half her own weight, live on forage that might have starved a goat, and smell water fifteen miles in time of drought. Speed was not in her vocabulary, and accordingly it was late afternoon rather than morning when Gregg, pointing his course between the ears of Mame, steered her through Murphy's Pass and came out over Alder. There they paused by mutual consent, and the burro flicked one long ear forward to listen to the rushing of the Doane River. It filled the valley with continual murmur, and just below them, where the brown, white-flecked current twisted around an elbow bend, lay Alder tossed down without plan, here a boulder and there a house. They seemed marvelously flimsy structures, and one felt surprise that the weight of the winter snow had not crushed them, or that the Doane River had not sent a strong current licking over the bank and tossed the whole village crashing down the ravine. One building was very much like another, but Gregg's familiar eye pierced through the roofs and into Widow Sullivan's staggering shack, into Hezekiah Whittleby's hushed sitting-room, down to the moist, dark floor of the Captain's saloon into that amazing junkshop, the General Merchandise store; but first and last he looked to the little flag which gleamed and snapped above the schoolhouse, and it spelled "my country" to Vic.

Mame consented to break into a neat-footed jog-trot going down the last slope, and so she went up the single winding street of Alder, grunting at every step, with Gregg's whistle behind her. In town, he lived with his friend, Dug Pym, who kept their attic room reserved for his occupancy, so he headed straight for that place. What human face would he see first?

It was Mrs. Sweeney's little boy, Jack, who raced into the street whooping, and Vic caught him under the armpits and swung him dizzily into the air.

"By God," muttered Vic, as he strode on, "that's a good kid, that Jack." And he straightway forgot all about that knife which Jackie had purloined from him the summer before. "Me and Betty," he thought, "we'll have kids like Jack; tougher'n leather."

Old Garrigan saw him next and cackled from his truck garden in the backyard, but Vic went on with a wave of his arm, and on past Gertie Vincent's inviting shout (Gertie had been his particular girl before Betty Neal came to town), and on with the determination of a soldier even past the veranda of Captain Lorrimer's saloon, though Lorrimer himself bellowed a greeting and "Chick" Stewart crooked a significant thumb over his shoulder towards the open door. He only paused at the blacksmith shop and looked in at Dug, who was struggling to make the print of a hot shoe on a hind foot of Simpson's sorrel Glencoe.

"Hey, Dug!"

Pym raised a grimy, sweating forehead.

"You, boy; easy, damn you! Hello, Vic!" and he propped that restless hind foot on his inner thigh and extended a hand.

"Go on workin', Dug, because I can't stop; I just want a rope to catch Grey Molly."

"You red devil!—take that rope over there, Vic. You won't have no work catchin' Molly. Which she's plumb tame. Stand still, damn you. I never seen a Glencoe with any sense!—Where you goin', Vic? Up to the school?"

And his sweaty grin followed Vic as the latter went out with the coil of rope over his shoulder. When Gregg reached the house. Nelly Pym hugged him, which is the privilege of fat and forty, and then she sat at the foot of the stairs and shouted up gossip while he shaved with

13

frantic haste and jumped into his best clothes. He answered her with monosyllables and only half his mind.

"Finish up your work, Vic?"

"Nope."

"You sure worked yourself all thin. I hope somebody appreciates it." She chuckled. "Ain't been sick, have you?"

"Nope."

"Say, who d'you think's in town? Sheriff Glass!"

This information sank in on him while he tugged at a boot at least a size and half too small.

"Pete Glass!" he echoed. Then: "Who's he after?"

"I dunno. Vic, he don't look like such a bad one."

"He's plenty bad enough," Gregg assured her. "Ah-h-h!" His foot ground into place, torturing his toes.

"Well," considered Mrs. Pym, in a philosophic rumble, "I s'pose them quiet gents is the dangerous ones, mostly; but looking at Glass you wouldn't think he'd ever killed all those men. Know about the dance?"

"Nope."

"Down to Singer's place. Betty goin' with you?"

He jerked open the door and barked down at her: "Who else would she be goin' with?"

"Don't start pullin' leather before the hoss bucks," said Mrs. Pym. "*I* don't know who else she'd be goin' with. You sure look fine in that red shirt, Vic!"

He grinned, half mollified, half shame-faced, and ducked back into the room, but a moment later he clumped stiffly down the stairs, frowning. He wondered if he could dance in those boots.

"Feel kind of strange in these clothes. How do I look, Nelly?" And he turned in review at the foot of the stairs.

"Slick as a whistle, I'll tell a man." She raised her voice to a shout as he disappeared through the outer door. "Kiss her once for me, Vic."

In the center of the little pasture he stood shaking out the noose, and the three horses raced in a sweeping gallop around the fence, looking for a place of escape, with Grey Molly in the lead. Nothing up the Doane River, or even down the Asper, for that matter, could head Molly when she was full of running, and the eyes of Gregg gleamed as he watched her. She was not a picture horse,

14

for her color was rather a dirty white than a dapple, and besides, there were some who accused her of "tucked up belly." But she had the legs for speed in spite of the sloping croup, and plenty of chest at the girth, and a small, bony head that rejoiced the heart of a horseman. He swung the noose, and while the others darted ahead, straight into the range of danger, Grey Molly whirled like a doubling coyote and leaped away.

"Good girl!" cried Vic, in involuntary approbation. He ran a few steps. The noose slid up and out, opened in a shaky loop, and swooped down. Too late the gray saw the flying danger, for even as she swerved the riata fell over her head, and she came to a snorting halt with all fours planted, skidding through the grass. The first thing a range horse learns is never to pull against a rope.

A few minutes later she was getting the "pitch" out of her system, as any self-respecting cattle horse must do after a session of pasture and no work. She bucked with enthusiasm and intelligence, as she did all things. Sun-fishing, Sun-fishing is the most deadly form of bucking, for it consists of a series of leaps apparently aimed at the sun, and the horse comes down with a sickening jar on stiff front legs. Educated "pitchers" land on only one foot, so that the shock is accompanied by a terrible sidewise, downward wrench that breaks the hearts of the best riders in the world. Grey Molly was educated, and Mrs. Pym stood in the doorway with a broad grin of appreciation on her red face, she knew riding when she saw it. Then, out of the full frenzy, the mare lapsed into high-headed, quivering attention, and Gregg cursed her softly, with deep affection. He understood her from her fetlocks to her teeth. She bucked like a field of revolt one instant and cantered like an angel of grace the next; in fact, she was more or less of an equine counterpart of her rider.

But now he heard shrill voices passing down the street and he knew that school was out and that he must hurry if he wanted to ride home with Betty, so he waved to Mrs. Pym and cantered away. For over two days he had been rushing towards this meeting; all winter he had hungered for it; but now that the moment loomed before him he weakened; he usually did when he came close to the girl.

15

Not that her beauty overwhelmed him, for though she had a portion of energetic good-health and freckled prettiness, he had chosen her as an Indian chooses flint for his steel; one could strike fire from Betty Neal. When he was far away he loved her without doubt or question and his trust ran towards her like a river setting towards the ocean because he knew that her heart was a big and as true as the heart of Grey Molly herself. Only her ways were fickle, and when he came near, she filled him with uneasiness, suspicion.

CHAPTER III

~Battle

On the road he passed Miss Brewster—for the Alder school boasted two teachers!—and under her kindly, rather faded smile he felt a great desire to stop and take her into his confidence; ask her what Betty Neal had been doing all these months. Instead, he touched Grey Molly with the spurs, and she answered like a watch-spring uncurling beneath him. The rush of wind against his face raised his spirits to a singing pitch, and when he flung from the saddle before the school he shouted: "Oh, Betty!"

Up the sharply angling steps in a bound, and at the door: "Oh, Betty!"

His voice filled the room with a thick, dull echo, and there was Betty behind her desk looking up at him agape; and beside her stood Blondy Hansen, big, good-looking, and equally startled. Fear made the glance of Vic Gregg swerve to where little Tommy Aiken scribbled an arithmetic problem on the blackboard—after-school work for whispering in class, or some equally heinous crime. The tingling voices of the other children, on their way home, floated in to Tommy, and the corners of his mouth drooped.

To regain his poise, Vic tugged at his belt and felt the weight of the holster slipping into a more convenient place, then he sauntered up the aisle, sweeping off his sombrero. Every feeling in his body, every nerve, disappeared in a crystalline hardness, for it seemed to him that the air was surcharged by a secret something between Betty and young Hansen. Betty was out from behind her desk and she ran to meet him and took his hand in both

17

of hers. The rush of her coming took his breath, and at her touch something melted in her.

"Oh, Vic, are you all through?"

Gregg stiffened for the benefit of Hansen and Tommy Aiken.

"Pretty near through," he said carelessly. "Thought I'd drop down to Alder for a day or two and get the kinks out. Hello, Blondy. Hey, Tommy!"

Tommy Aiken flashed a grin at him, but Tommy was not quite sure that the rules permitted speaking, even under such provocation as the return of Vic Gregg, so he maintained a desperate silence. Blondy had picked up his hat as he returned the greeting.

"I guess I'll be going," he said, and coughed to show that he was perfectly at ease, but it seemed to Vic that it was hard for Blondy to meet his eye when they shook hands. "See you later, Betty."

"All right." She smiled at Vic—a flash—and then gathered dignity of both voice and manner. "You may go now, Tommy."

She lapsed into complete unconsciousness of manner as Tommy swooped on his desk, included hat and book in one grab, and darted towards the door through which Hansen had just disappeared. Here he paused, tilting, and his smile twinkled at them with understanding. "Good-night, Miss Neal. Hope you have a good time, Vic." His heel clicked twice on the steps outside, and then the patter of his racing feet across the field.

"The little mischief!" said Betty, delightfully flushed. "It beats everything, Vic, how Alder takes things for granted."

He should have taken her in his arms and kissed her, now that she had cleared the room, he very well knew, but the obvious thing was always last to come in Gregg's repertoire.

"Why not take it for granted? It ain't going to be many days, now."

He watched her eyes sparkle, but the pleasure of seeing him drowned the gleam almost at once.

"Are you really almost through? Oh, Vic, you've been

away so long, and I——" She checked herself. There was no overflow of sentiment in Betty.

"Maybe I was a fool for laying off work this way," he admitted, "but I sure got terrible lonesome up there."

Her glance went over him contentedly, from the hard brown hands to the wrinkle which labor had sunk in the exact center of his forehead. He was all man, to Betty.

Come on along," he said. He would kiss her by surprise as they reached the door. "Come on along. It's sure enough spring outside. I been eating it up, and—we can do our talking over things at the dance. Let's ride now."

"Dance?"

"Sure, down to Singer's place."

"It's going to be kind of hard to get out of going with Blondy. He asked me."

"And you said you'd go?"

"What are you flarin' up about?"

"Look here, how long have you been traipsin' around with Blondy Hansen?"

She clenched one hand beside her in a way he knew, but it pleased him more than it warned him, just as it pleased him to see the ears of Grey Molly go back.

"What's wrong about Blondy Hansen?"

"What's right about him?" he countered senselessly.

Her voice went a bit shrill. "Blondy is a gentleman, I'll have you know."

"Is he?"

"Don't you sneer at me, Victor Gregg. I won't have it!"

"You won't, eh?"

He felt that he was pushing her to the danger point, but she was perfectly, satisfyingly beautiful in her anger; he taunted her with the pleasure of an artist painting a picture.

"I won't!" she repeated. Something else came to her lips, but she repressed it, and he could see the pressure from within telling.

"Don't get in a huff over nothing," he urged, in real alarm. "Only, it made me kind of mad to see Blondy standing there with that calf-look."

"What calf-look? He's a lot better to look at than you'll ever be."

A smear of red danced before the vision of Gregg.

"I don't set up for no beauty prize. Tie a pink ribbon in Blondy's hair and take him to a baby show if you want. He's about young enough to enter."

If she could have found a ready retort her anger might have passed away in words, but no words came and she turned pale. It was here that Gregg made his crucial mistake, for he thought the pallor came from fear, fear which his sham jealousy had roused in her, perhaps. He should have maintained a discreet silence, but instead, he poured in the gall of complacency upon a raw wound.

"Blondy's all right," he stated beneficently, "but you just forget about him to-night. You're going to that dance and you're going with me. If there's any explanations to be made, you leave 'em to me. I'll handle Blondy."

"You handle Blondy!" she whispered. Her voice came back; it rang: "You couldn't if he had one hand tied behind him." She measured him for another blow. "I'm going to that dance and I'm going with Mr. Hansen."

She knew that he would have died for her, and he knew that she would have died for him; accordingly they abandoned themselves to sullen fury.

"You're out of date, Vic," she ran on. "Men can't drag women around nowadays, and you can't drag me. Not—one—inch." She put a vicious little interval between each of the last three words.

"I'll be calling for you at seven o'clock."

"I won't be there."

"Then I'll call on Blondy."

"You don't dare to. Don't you try to bluff me. I'm not that kind."

"Betty, d'you mean that? D'you think that I'm yaller?"

"I don't care what you are."

"I ask you calm and impersonal, just think that over before you say it."

"I've already thought it over."

"Then, By God," said Gregg, trembling, "I'll never take one step out of my way to see you again."

He turned, so blind with fury that he shouldered the door on his way out and so, into the saddle, with Grey Molly standing like a figure of rock, as if she sensed his mood. He swung her about on her hind legs with a wrench on the curb and a lift of his spurs, but when she leaped into a gallop he brought her back to a walk with a cruel jerk; she began to sidle across the field with her chin drawn almost back to her breast, prancing. The movement of the horse brought him half way around towards the door and he was tempted mightily to look, for he knew that Betty Neal was standing there, begging him with her eyes. But the great, sullen pain conquered; he straightened out the mare for the gate.

Betty was indeed at the door, leaning against it in a sudden weakness, and even in her pain she felt pride in the grace and skill of Vic's horsemanship. The hearts of both of them were breaking, with this rather typical difference: that Gregg felt her to be entirely at fault, and that she as fully accepted every scruple of the blame. He had come down tired out and nervous from work he had done for her sake, she remembered, and if he would only glance back once—he must know that she was praying for it—she would crop out and run down to him; but he went on, on, through the gate.

A flash of her passion returned to her. "I *shall* go with Blondy—if it kills me." And she flung herself into the nearest seat and wept.

So when he reached the road and looked back at last, the doorway yawned black, empty, and he set his teeth with a groan and spurred down the road for Alder. He drew rein at Captain Lorrimer's and entered with curt nods in exchange for the greetings.

"Red-eye," he ordered, and seized bottle and glass as Lorrimer spun them deftly towards him.

Captain Lorrimer picked up the bottle and gazed at it mournfully when Vic had poured his drink.

"Son," he murmured, "you've sure raised an awful thirst."

CHAPTER IV

King Hol

There is a very general and very erroneous impression that alcohol builds the mood of a man; as a matter of fact it merely makes his temper of the moment fast—the man who takes his first drink with a smile ends in uproarious laughter, and he who frowns will often end in fighting. Vic Gregg did not frown as he drank, but the corners of his lips turned up a trifle in a smile of fixed and acid pleasantry and his glance went from face to face in the barroom, steadily, with a trifling pause at each pair of eyes. Beginning with himself, he hated mankind in general; the burn of the cheap whisky within served to set the color of that hatred in a fixed dye. He did not lift his chaser, but his hand closed around it hard. If some one had given him an excuse for a fist-fight or an outburst of cursing it would have washed his mind as clean as a new slate, and five minutes later he might have been with Betty Neal, riotously happy. Instead, every one overflowed with good nature, gossip, questions about his work, and the danger in him crystallized. He registered cold reasons for his disgust.

Beginning in the first person, he loathed himself as a thick-headed ass for talking to Betty as he had done; as well put a burr under one's saddle and then feel surprise because the horse bucks. He passed on to the others with equal precision. Captain Lorrimer was as dirty as a greaser; and like a greaser, loose-lipped, unshaven. Chick Stewart was a born fool, and a fool by self-culture, as his never changing grin amply proved. Lew Perkins sat in the corner on a shaky old apple barrel and brushed back his long mustaches to spit at the cuspidor—

and miss it. If this were Vic Gregg's saloon he would teach the old loafer more accuracy or break his neck.

"How are you, Gregg?" murmured some one behind him.

He turned and found Sheriff Pete Glass with his right hand already spread on the bar while he ordered a drink for two. That was one of the sheriff's idiosyncracies; he never shook hands if he could avoid it, and Gregg hated him senselessly, bitterly, for it. No doubt every one in the room noticed, and they would tell afterwards how the sheriff had avoided shaking hands with Vic Gregg. Cheap play for notoriety, thought Gregg; Glass was pushing the bottle towards him.

"Help yourself," said Gregg.

"This is on me, Vic."

"I most generally like to buy the first drink."

Pete Glass turned his head slowly, for indeed all his motions were leisurely and one could not help wondering at the stories of his exploits, the tales of his hair-trigger alertness. Perhaps these half legendary deeds sent the thrill of uneasiness through Vic Gregg; perhaps it was owing to the singular hazel eyes, with little splotches of red in them; very mild eyes, but one could imagine anything about them. Otherwise there was nothing exceptional in Glass, for he stood well under middle height, a starved figure, with a sinewy crooked neck, as if bent on looking up to taller men. His hair was sandy, his face tamny brown, his shirt a gray blue, and every one knew his dusty roan horse; by nature, by temperament and by personal selection he was suited to blend into a landscape of sage-dotted plains or sand. Tireless as a lobo on the trail, swift as a bobcat in fight, hunted men had been known to ride in and give themselves up when they heard that Pete Glass was after them.

"Anyway you want, partner," he was saying, in his soft, rather husky voice.

He poured his drink, barely enough to cover the bottom of his glass, for that was another of Pete's ways; he could never afford to weaken his hand or deaden his eye with alcohol, and even now he stood sideways at the bar, facing Gregg and also facing the others in the room.

But the larger man, with sudden scorn for this caution, brimmed his own glass, and poised it swiftly. "Here's how!" and down it went.

Ordinarily red-eye heated his blood and made his brain dizzy, it loosened his tongue and numbed his lips, but today it left him cool, confident, and sharpened his vision until he felt that he could see through the minds of every one in the room. Captain Lorrimer, for instance, was telling a jocular story to Chick Stewart in the hope that Chick would set them up for every one; and old Lew Perkins was waiting for the treat; and perhaps the sheriff was wondering how he could handle Vic in case of need, or how long it would take to run him down. Not long, decided Gregg, breathing hard; no man in the world could put him on the run. Glass was treating in turn, and again the brimming drink went down Vic's throat and left his brain clear, wonderfully clear. He saw through Betty Neal now; she had purposely played off Blondy against him, to make them both jealous.

"Won't you join us, Dad?" the sheriff was saying to Lew Perkins, and Vic Gregg smiled. He understood. The sheriff wanted an excuse to order another round of drinks because he had it in mind to intoxicate Gregg; perhaps Glass had something on him; perhaps the manhunter thought that Vic had had a part in that Wilsonville affair two years back. That was it, he wanted to make Vic talk when he was drunk.

"Don't mind if I do," Lew said, slapping both hands on the bar as if he owned it; and while he waited for his drink: "What are you going to do with Swain?"

The doddering idiot! Swain was the last man Glass had taken, and Lew Perkins should have known that the sheriff never talked about his work; the old ass was in his green age, his second childhood.

"Swain turned state's evidence," said Pete, curtly. "He'll go free, I suppose. Fill up your glass, partner. I can see you're thirsty yet."

This was to Gregg who had purposely poured out a drink of the sheriff's own chosen dimension to see if the latter would notice; this remark fixed his suspicions. It was certain that the manhunter was after him, but again, in scorn, he accepted the challenge and poured a stiff dram.

"That's right," nodded the sheriff. "You got nothing on your shoulders. You can let yourself go, Vic. Sometimes I wish"—he sighed—"I wish I could do the same!"

"The sneaky coyote," thought Gregg, "he's lurin' me on!"

"Turned state's evidence!" maundered Lew Perkins. "Well, they's a lot of 'em that lose their guts when they're caught. I remember way back in the time when Bannack was runnin' full blast——"

Why did not some one shut off the old idiot before he was thoroughly started? He might keep on talking like the clank of a windmill in a steady breeze, endlessly. For Lew was old—seventy-five, eighty, eighty-five—he himself probably did not know just how old—and he had lived through at least two generations of pioneers with a myriad stories about them. He could string out tales of the Long Trail: Abilene, Wichita, Ellsworth, Great Bend, Newton, where eleven men were murdered in one night; he knew the vigilante days in San Francisco, and early times in Alder Gulch.

"Nobody would of thought Plummer was yaller, but he turned out that way," droned on the narrator. "Grit?" He had enough to fit out twenty men. When Crawford shot him and busted his right arm, he went right on and learned to shoot with his left and started huntin' Jack again. Packed that lead with him till he died, and then they found Jack's bullet in his wrist, all worked smooth by the play of the bones. Afterwards it turned out that Plummer ran a whole gang; but before we learned that we'd been fools enough to make him sheriff. We got to Plummer right after he'd finished hangin' a man, and took him to his own gallows.

"You'd of thought a cool devil like that would of made a good end, but he didn't. He just got down on his knees and cried, and asked God to help him. Then he begged us to give him time to pray, but one of the boys up and told him he could do his prayin' from the cross-beam. And that was Henry Plummer, that killed a hundred men, him an' his gang."

"H-m-m," murmured the sheriff, and looked uneasily about. Now that his eyes were turned away, Vic could study him at leisure, and he wondered at the smallness of the man. Suppose one were able to lay hands on him it would be easy to——

"See you later, boys," drawled Glass and sauntered from the room.

Lew Perkins sighed as the most important part of his audience disappeared, but having started talking the impetus carried him along, he held Vic Gregg with his hazy eyes.

"But they didn't all finish like Plummer, not all the bad ones. No sirree! There was Boone Helm."

"I've heard about him," growled Vic, but the old man had fixed his glance and his reminiscent smile upon the past and his voice was soft with distance when he spoke again.

"Helm was a sure enough bad one, son. They don't grow like him no more. Wild Bill was a baby compared with Helm, and Slade wasn't no man at all, even leavin' in the lies they tell about him. Why, son, Helm was just a lobo in the skin of a man——"

"Like Larry?" put in Lorrimer, drifting closer down the bar.

"Who's he?"

"Aint you heard of Whistlin' Dan? The one that killed Jim Silent and busted up his gang. Why, they say he's got a wolf that he can talk to like it was a man."

Old Lew chuckled.

"They say a lot of things," he nodded, "but I'll tell a man that a wolf is a wolf and they ain't nothin' that can tame 'em. Don't you let 'em feed you up on lies like that, Lorrimer. But Helm was sure bad. He killed for the sake of killin', but he died game. When the boys run him down he swore on the bible that he's never killed a man, and they made him swear it over again just to watch his nerve; but he never batted an eye."

The picture of that wild time grew up for Vic Gregg, and the thought of free men who laughed at the law, strong men, fierce men. What would one of these have done if the girl he intended to marry had treated him like a foil?

"Then they got him ready for the rope," went on Lew Perkins.

" 'I've seen a tolerable lot of death,' says Helm. 'I ain't afraid of it.'

"There was about six thousand folks had come in to see the end of Boone Helm. Somebody asked him if he wanted anything.

" 'Whisky,' says Boone. And he got it.

"Then he shook his hand and held it up. He had a sore finger and it bothered him a lot more than the thought of hangin'.

" 'You gents get through with this or else tie up my finger,' he kept sayin'.

"Helm wasn't the whole show. There was some others bein' hung that day and when one of them dropped off his box, Boone says: 'There's one gone to hell.' Pretty soon another went, and hung there wiggling, and six times he went through all the motions of pullin' his six-shooter and firin' it. I counted. "Kick away, old fellow,' says Boone Helm, 'I'll be with you soon.' Then it came his turn and he hollered: 'Hurrah for Jeff Davis; let her rip!' That was how Boone Helm——"

The rest of the story was blotted from the mind of Vic Gregg by the thud of a heavy heel on the veranda, and then the broad shoulders of Blondy Hansen darkened the doorway, Blondy Hansen dressed for the dance, with the knot of his black silk handkerchief turned to the front and above that the gleam of his celluloid collar. It was dim in the saloon, compared with the brightness of the outdoors, and perhaps Blondy did not see Vic. At any rate he took his place at the other end of the bar. Three pictures tangled in the mind of Gregg like three bodies in a whirlpool—Betty, Blondy, Pete Glass. That strange clearness of perception increased and the whole affair lay plainly before him. Betty had sent Hansen, dressed manifestly for the festival, to gloat over Vic in Lorrimer's place. He was at it already.

"All turned out for the dance, Blondy, eh? Takin' a girl?"

27

"Betty Neal," answered Blondy.

"The hell you are!" inquired Lorrimer, mildly astonished. "I thought—why, Vic's back in town, don't you know that?"

"He ain't got a mortgage on what she does."

Then, guided by the side-glance of Lorrimer, Hansen saw Gregg, and he stiffened. As for Vic, he perceived the last link in his chain of evidence. Hansen was going to a dance, and yet he wore a gun, and there could be only one meaning in that: Betty had sent him down there to wind up the affair.

"Didn't see you, Vic," Blondy was saying, his flushed face seemingly doubly red against the paleness of his hair. "Have something?"

"I ain't drinkin'," answered Gregg, and slowly, to make sure that no one could miss his meaning, he poured out a glass of liquor, and drank it with his face towards Hansen. When he put his glass down his mind was clearer than ever; and with omniscient precision, with nerveless calm, he knew that he was going to kill Blondy Hansen; knew exactly where the bullet would strike. It was something put behind him; his mind had already seen Hansen fall, and he smiled.

Dead silence had fallen over the room, and in the silence Gregg heard a muffled, ticking sound, the beating of his heart; heard old Lew Perkins as the latter softly, slowly, glided back out of the straight line of danger; heard the quick breathing of Captain Lorrimer who stood pasty pale, gaping behind the bar; heard the gritted teeth of Blondy Hansen, who would not take water.

"Vic," said Blondy, "it looks like you mean trouble. Anyway, you just now done something that needs explaining."

He stood straight as a soldier, rigid, but the fingers of his right hand twitched, twitched, twitched; the hand itself stole higher. Very calmly, Vic hunted for his words, found them.

"A cattle rustler is bad," he pronounced, "a hoss thief is worse, but you're the lowest sneak of the lot, Blondy."

Again that silence with the pulse in it, and Vic Gregg

28

could feel the chill which numbed every one except himself.

The lower jaw of Captain Lorrimer sagged, and his whisper came out in jerking syllables: "God Almighty!" Then Blondy went for his gun, and Vic waited with his hand on the butt of his own, waited with a perfect, cold foreknowledge, heard Blondy moan as his Colt hung in the holster, saw the flash of the barrel as it whipped out, and then jerked his own weapon and fired from the hip. Blondy staggered but kept himself from falling by gripping the edge of the bar with his left hand; the right, still holding the gun, raised and rubbed across his forehead; he looked like a sleeper awakening.

Not a sound from any one else, while Vic watched the tiny wraith of smoke jerk up from the muzzle of his revolver. Then Blondy's gun flashed down and clanked on the floor. A red spot grew on the breast of Hansen's shirt; now he leaned as if to pick up something, but instead, slid forward on his face. Vic stepped to him and stirred the body with his toe; it wobbled, limp.

CHAPTER V

The Flight

There were three spots of white in the dim saloon, the faces of Stewart, Lorrimer, and old Lew Perkins, and at the feet of Vic grew a spot of red. Knowing with calm surety that no hand would lift against him even if he turned his back, he walked out the door without a word and swung into the saddle. There, for an instant, he calculated chances, for the street stretched empty before and behind with not a sound of warning stirring in the saloon. He was greatly tempted to ride to Dug Pym's for his blanket roll and a few other traveling necessities, but he remembered that the men of Alder rose to action with astonishing speed; within five minutes a group of hard riders would be clattering up his trail with Pete Glass at their head. An unlucky Providence had sent Pete to Alder on this day of all days. There stood his redoubtable dusty roan at the hitching rack, her head low, one ear back and one flopped forward, her under lip pendulous—in a pasture full of horses one might pick her last either for stout heart or speed. Even in spite of her history Vic would have engaged Grey Molly to beat the roan at equal weights, but since he outbulked the sheriff full forty pounds, he weighed in nice balance the necessity of shooting the roan before he left Alder. It was, he decided, unpleasant but vital, and his fingers had already slid around the butt of his gun when a horse whinnied far off and the roan twitched up her head to listen. She was no longer a cloddish lump of horseflesh, but an individual, a soul; Gregg's hand fell from his gun. Cursing his sentimental weakness, he lifted Molly into a canter down the street. Still no signs of awakening behind him or about;

only little Jack Sweeney playing tag with a black-and-tan puppy, the triumphant cackle of a hen somewhere to the left; but as he neared the end of the street, where the trail swung into the rocks of the slope, a door banged far off and a voice was screaming: "Pete! Pete Glass!"

Grey Molly switched her tail nervously at the shout, but Vic was too wise to let her waste strength hurrying up so sharp a declivity; that dusty roan whose life he had spared would be spending it prodigally to overtake him before long and Molly's power must be husbanded. So he kept her at a quick walk by pressing the calf of one leg into her flank and turned in the saddle to watch the town sink behind him. Sometime in the vague, stupid past Mame had jog-trotted down this slope, but now he was a new man with an eye which saw all things and a gun which could not fail. Figures, singularly tiny and singularly distinct, swarmed into the street from nowhere, men on horses, men swinging into saddles; here and there the slant light of the afternoon twinkled on gun barrels, and ludicrous thin voices came piping up the hill. As he reached the nether lip of Murphy's Pass a small cavalcade detached itself from the main mass before Captain Lorrimer's saloon and swept down the street, first a dusty figure on a dusty horse, hardly visible; then a spot of red which must be Harry Fisher on his blood-bay, with a long-striding sorrel beside him that could carry no one except grim old Slivers Waldron. Behind these rode one with the light glinting on his silver conchos—Mat Henshaw, the town Beau Brummel—then the black Guss Reeve, and last of all "Ronicky" Joe on his pinto; "Ronicky" Joe, handy man at all things, and particularly guns. It showed how fast Pete Glass could work and how well he knew Alder, for Vic himself could not have selected five cooler fighters among the villagers or five finer mounts. The posse switched around the end of the street and darted up the hill like the curling lash of a whip.

"Good," said Vic Gregg. "The damn fools will wind their horses before they hit the pass."

He put Grey Molly into an easy trot, for the floor of the pass dipped up and down, littered with sharp-toothed rocks or treacherous, rolling ones, as bad a place for

31

speed as a stiff up-slope. According to his nicest calculation the posse could not reach the edge of the gulch before he was at the farther side, out of range of everything except a long chance shot, so he took note of things as he went and observed a spot of pale silver skirting through the brush on the eastern ridge of the gorge. There would be moonlight that night and another chance in favor of Pete Glass. He remembered then, with quiet content, that jogging in the holster was a power which with six words might stop those six pursuers.

A long halloo came barking down the pass, now drawling out, now cut away to silence as the angling cliffs sent on the echo, and Vic loosened the rein. Grey Molly swung out with a snort of relief to a free-swinging gallop and they swept down a great, gentle slope where new grass padded the fall of her hoofs, yet even then he kept the mare checked and held her in touch with an easily playing wrist. He did not imagine that even the sheriff on the dusty roan would dream of trying to swallow up Grey Molly in a short sprint but that assurance nearly cost Vic his life. The roar of hoofs in the gulch belched out into the comparative silence of the open space beyond and just as he gave the mare her head a gun coughed and an angry humming darted past his ear.

Molly lengthened into full speed. He could not tell on account of the muffling grass whether the pursuit was gaining or losing. He trusted blindly to the mare and when he looked back they were already pulling their mounts down to a hand gallop. That would teach them to match Molly in a sprint, roan or no roan!

He slapped her below the withers, where the long, hard muscles rippled back and forth. She was full of running, her gallop as light as the toss of a bough in the wind, and now as he pulled her back to a swinging canter her head went high, with pricking ears. Suddenly his heart went out to her; she would run like that till she died, he knew.

"Good girl," he whispered huskily.

The day was paling towards the end when he headed into the foothills of the White Mountains. He drew up Molly for a breath on a level shoulder. Already he was close to the snow line with ragged heads of white rearing above him. Far below, a pale streak of moonlight was the Asper. Then, out of that blacker night on the slopes beneath, he heard the clinking hoofs of the posse; the quiet was so perfect, the air so clear, that he even caught the chorus of straining saddle-leather and then voices of men. All this time the effects of the whisky had been wearing away by imperceptible degrees and at that sound all his old self rushed back on Vic Gregg. Why, they were his friends, his partners, these voices in the night, and that clear laughter floated up from Harry Fisher who had been his bunkie at the Circle V Bar ranch three years ago. He felt an insane impulse to lean over the edge of the cliff and shout a greeting.

CHAPTER VI

The Rifle

Dawn found him over the first crest; at noon he was struggling up the slope of the second range, whose rise was not half so sharp as the upward plunge out of the Asper, but in spite of that easier ground Grey Molly could not gain. She went with shorter steps, now, and her head hung lower and lower, yet when a down stretch opened before her she went at it with a gallop as light, almost, as her race out of Murphy's Pass. Not once had she offered to stop; not once had she winced from the labor of some sharp up-pitch; but still six horsemen hung behind her, and at their head rode a little dusty man on a little dusty roan. It was the lack of training as well as the rough going which held Molly back.

Beyond that second range, however, the down slope stretched smoothly, evenly, for mile on mile and mile on mile; perfect going for Grey Molly over easy hills with patches of forest here and there where he might double, or where he might stop with the hunt sweeping past. All this the sheriff must have known perfectly well, for he no longer kept back with his pack of five, but skirted on ahead, hunting alone. Again and again Vic heard the little shrill whistle with which Pete Glass encouraged the roan. Vic used the spurs twice, and then he desisted from the useless brutality for Molly was doing her best and no power on earth could make her do more. After all, her best would be good enough, for now Vic looked up and his heart leaped into his throat; there was only one more rise above him, and beyond lay the easy ground and a running chance for Molly's slender legs. Even as he raised his head something whined evilly over him, followed by a

34

sound like two heavy hammers swung together, face to face, and shattered by the stroke. A rifle!

He looked back, saw the roan standing broadside towards him, watched the sun waver and then flash in a straight steady line along the barrel of the sheriff's gun. The line of light jerked up, and before the sound reached him a blow on his right shoulder sent Vic lurching forward against the pommel. Afterwards the voice of the rifle rang around him and a sharp pain twitched up and down his side, then ran tingling to his fingertips.

It was the stunning blow which saved him, for the sheriff had the range and his third bullet would have clipped Vic between the shoulders, but Glass had seen his quarry pitch forward in the saddle and he would not waste ammunition. The thrift of his New England ancestry spoke in Pete now and then and he could only grit his teeth when he saw Vic, disappearing on the other side of the crest, straighten in the saddle; the next instant the top of the hill shielded the fugitive.

Well and nobly, then, Grey Molly repaid all the praise, all the tenderness and care which Vic had lavished upon her in the past years, for with her legs shaking from the struggle of that last climb, with a rider who wobbled crazily in his seat, with reins hanging loose on her neck, with not even a voice to guide or to encourage her, she swept straight across the falling ground, gaining strength and courage at every stride. By the time Vic had regained his self-control and rallied a little from that first terrible falling of the heart, the dusty roan was over the crest and streaking after the game. Grey Molly gained steadily, yet even when he gathered the reins in his left hand Vic knew that the fight was done, in effect. How could he double or dodge when his own blood spotted the trail he kept, and how long could he keep the saddle with the agony which tore like saw-teeth at his shoulder?

Grey Molly plunged straight into the shadow of pine trees, and the cool gloom fell like a blessing upon Vic in his torment; it was heaven to be sheltered even for a few moments from the eyes of the posse. At the opposite edge of the wood he drew rein with a groan. Some devil had prompted Gus Reeve and some devil had poured

Reeve's horse full of strength, for yonder down the valley, not a hundred yards away, galloped a rider on a black horse; yet Vic could have sworn that when he looked back from the crest he had seen Gus riding the very last in the posse. An instant later the illusion vanished, for the black horse of Gus was never an animal such as this, never had this marvelous, long gait. Its feet flicked the earth and shot it along with a reaching stride so easy, so flowing that only the fluttered mane and tail stretching straight behind gave token of the speed. For the rest, it carried its head high, with pricking ears, the sure sign of a horse running well within his strength; yet Grey Molly, fresh and keen for racing, could hardly have kept pace with the black as it slid over the hills. God in heaven, if such a horse were his a thousand sheriffs on a thousand dusty roans could never take him; five minutes would sweep him out of sight and reach.

Before the horseman ran a tall dog, wolfish in head and wolfish in the gait which carried it like a cloud-shadow over the ground, but it was over-large for any wolf Vic had ever seen. It turned its head now, and leaped aside at sight of the stranger, but the rider veered from his course and swept down on Vic. He came to a halt close up without either a draw at the reins or a spoken word, probably controlling his mount with pressure of the knees, and Gregg found himself facing a delicately handsome fellow. He was neither cowpuncher nor miner. Vic knew at a glance, for that face had never been haggard with labor. A tenderfoot, probably in spite of his dress, and Vic felt that if his right arm were sound he could take that horse at the point of his gun and leave the rider thanking God that his life had been spared; but his left hand was useless on the butt of a revolver, and three minutes away came the posse, racing. There was only time for one desperate appeal.

"Stranger," he burst out, "I'm follered. I got to have your hoss. Take this one in exchange; it's the best I ever threw a leg over. Here's two hundred bucks——" he flung his wallet on the ground and swung himself out of the saddle.

The wolfish dog, which had growled softly all this

time and roughed up the hair of its neck, now slunk forward on its belly.

"Heel, Bart!" commanded the stranger sharply, and the dog whipped about and stood away, whining with eagerness.

The moment Gregg's feet struck the ground his legs buckled like saplings in a wind for the long ride had sapped his strength, and the flow of blood told rapidly on him now. The hills and trees whirled around him until a lean, strong hand caught him under either armpit. The stranger stood close.

"You could have my hoss if you could ride him," said he. His voice was singularly unhurried and gentle. "But you'd drop out of the saddle in ten minutes. Who's after you?"

A voice shouted, far off beyond the wood; another voice answered, nearer, and the whole soul of Gregg turned to the stallion. Grey Molly was blown, she stood now with hanging head and her flanks sunk in alarmingly at every breath, but even fresh from the pasture she was not a rag, not a straw compared to the black.

"For God's sake," groaned Vic, "*loan* me your hoss!"

"You couldn't stick the saddle. Come in here out of sight; I'm going to take 'em off your trail."

While he spoke, he led, half carried Vic, into a thicket of shrubs with a small open space at the center. The black and the wolf-dog followed and now the stranger pulled at the bridle rein. The stallion kneeled like a trained dog, and lying thus the shrubbery was high enough to hide him. Closer, sweeping through the wood, Vic heard the crash of the pursuit, yet the other was maddeningly slow of speech.

"You stay here, partner, and sit over there. I'm borrowin' your gun"—a swift hand appropriated it from Vic's holster and his own fingers were too paralyzed to resist— "and don't you try to ride my hoss unless you want them teeth in your throat. Lie quiet and tie up your hurt. Bart, watch him!"

And there sat Gregg where he had slipped down in his daze of weakness with the great dog crouched at his feet and snarling ominously every time he raised his hand. The voices came closer; the crashing burst on his very

37

ears, and now, through the interstices of the shrubbery he saw the stranger swing into the saddle on Grey Molly and urge her to a gallop. He could follow them for only an instant with his eyes, but it seemed to Vic that Molly cantered under her new rider with strange ease and lightness. It was partly the rest, no doubt, and partly the smaller burden.

A deep beat of racing hoofs, and then the dusty roan shot out of the trees close by with the sheriff leaning forward, jockeying his horse. It seemed that no living thing could escape from that relentless rider. Then right behind Vic a horse snorted and grunted—as it leaped a fallen log, perhaps—and he watched in alarm to see if the stallion would answer that sound with start or whinny. The black lay perfectly still, and instead of lifting up to answer or to look, the head lowered with ears flat back until the long, outstretched neck gave the animal a snaky appearance. The dog, too, though it showed murderous fangs whenever Vic moved, did not stir from his place, but lay flattening into the ground.

"Cut to the right! Cut to the right, Harry!" came the voice of the sheriff, already piping from the distance as the last of the posse brushed out from the trees. "Yo hoi! Gus, take the left arroyo!"

Two answering yells, and then the rush of hoofs fell away. They were cornering the stranger, no doubt, and Vic struggled to lift himself to his feet and watch until a faint sound from the dog made him look down. Bart lay with his haunches drawn up under him, his forepaws digging into the soft loam, his eyes demoniac. Instinctively Vic reached for his absent gun, and then, despairing, relaxed to his former position. The wolf-dog lowered his head to his paws and there remained with the eyes following each intake of Gregg's breath. A rattle of gun-shots flung back loosely from the hills, and among them Vic winced at the sound of the sheriff's rifle, clear and ringing over the bark of the revolvers.

Had they nailed the stranger? The firing recommenced, more faintly and prolonged, so that it was plain the posse maintained a running fusillade after the fugitive. After that fear of his own growing weakness shut out

38

all else from the mind of Gregg as he felt his senses, his physical strength, flowing out like an ebbtide to a sea which, he knew, was death. He began to work desperately to bind up the wound and stop the flow of blood and it was fear which gave him momentary strength to tear away his shirt and then with his teeth and left hand rip it into strips. After that, heedless of the pain, he constructed a rude bandage, very clumsily, for he had to work over his shoulder. Here his teeth, once more, were almost as useful as another hand, and as the bandage grew tight the deadly, warm trickle along his side lessened and his fingers fell away from the last knot. He fainted.

CHAPTER VII

Joan Disobeys

What he next knew was a fire of agony that wrapped his whole body and consciousness flashed back on him. Strong arms lifted him, up; above him he sensed the eyes of his torturer, dim in moonlight, and he beat his clubbed left fist into that face. After that he knew he was being dragged onto a saddle, but a wave of pain rushed up his side and numbed his brain. Thereafter his senses returned by fits and starts, vaguely. Once he felt a steel cable that girdled his waist and breast and held him erect, though his head flopped back and forth; once his eyes opened and above him glittered the bright field of stars toward which he drifted through space, a mind without a body; once a stab of torment wakened him enough to hear: "Easy Satan; watch them stones. One more jolt like that will send him clear to——" And the voice glided into an eternity of distance. Yet again he swung up from the pit of darkness and became aware of golden hair around a woman's face, and a marvelous soft, cool hand upon his forehead. Her voice reached him, too, and made him think of all things musical, all things distant, like the sounds of birds falling from the sky and though he understood not a syllable, a sweet assurance of safety flooded through him. He slept.

When he woke again, it was from a dream of fleeing through empty air swifter than the wind with a wolf-dog looming behind him out of space, but presently he found that he was lying in a bed with a stream of sunlight washing across a white coverlet. A door at his right swung open and there in the entrance stood the wolf-dog of his vision with a five-year-old girl upon its back.

"Don't go in there, Bart!" whispered the child. "Go on back!"

She took one of those pointed wolf-ears in her chubby fist and tugged to swing him around, but Bart, with a speed which the eye could not follow, twisted his head and the rows of great teeth closed over her hand. It was so horrible that the cry froze in the throat of Gregg, yet the child, with only a little murmur of anger, reached over with her other hand and caught the wolf by the nose.

"Bad Bart!" she whispered, and raised the hand which he instantly released. White marks showed on the pudgy tan. "Bad dog!" she repeated, and beat his neck with an impotent little fist. The wolf-dog cringed, and turned from the door.

"Come in," invited Gregg. He was surprised to find his voice thin, apt to swing up to a high pitch beyond his control. A shower of golden curls tossed away from her face as she looked at him. "Oh!" she cried, still with a guarded voice. She leaned far over, one hand buried in the ruff of Bart's neck to secure her balance, and with the other she laid hold of his right ear and drew him around facing the door once more. This time he showed his teeth but submitted, only twitching the ear back and forth a time or two when she relaxed her hold.

"Come in," repeated Gregg.

She canted her head to one side and considered him with fearless blue eyes.

"I want to," she sighed.

"Why can't you, honey?"

"Munner says no."

He attempted to turn further towards her, but the pain in his right shoulder prevented. He found that his arm was bandaged to the elbow and held close to his side by a complex swathing.

"Who is your mother?" asked Vic.

"Munner?" she repeated, frowning in wonder. "Why, munner is—my munner."

"Oh," smiled he, "and who's your pa?"

"What?"

41

"Who's your father? Who's your dad?"

"Daddy Dan. You ask a lot of things," she added, disapprovingly.

"Come on in," pleaded Vic Gregg, "and I won't ask nothin' more about you."

"Munner says no," she repeated.

She employed the moment of indecision by plucking at the hair of Bart's shoulders; he growled softly, terribly, but she paid not the slightest heed.

"Your mother won't care," asserted Vic.

"I know," she nodded, "but Daddy will."

"Spanking?"

She looked blankly at him.

"What will he do, then, if you come in to see me?"

"He'll look at me." She grew breathless at the thought, and cast a guilty glance over her shoulder.

"Honey," chuckled Gregg, weakly, "I'll take all the blame. Just you come along in and he'll do his lookin' at me."

He thought of the slender fellow who had rescued him and his large, gentle brown eyes, but to a child even those mild eyes might seem terrible with authority.

"Will you, true?" said the child, wistfully.

"Honest and true."

"All right." She made up her mind instantly, her face shining with excitement. "Giddap, Bart." And she thumped the wolf-dog vigorously with her heels.

He carried her in with a few gliding steps, soundless, except for the light rattle of claws on the floor, but he stopped well out of reach of the bed and when Vic held his left hand as far as he could across his chest, Bart winced and gave harsh warning. Vic had seen vicious dogs in his day, seen them fighting, seen them playing, but he had never heard one of them growl like this. The upper lips of the animal twitched dangerously back and the sound came from the very depths of his body. It made the flesh crawl along Vic's back; one rip of those great teeth could tear a man's throat open. The child thudded her heels against the ribs of Bart again.

"Giddap!" she cried.

The wolf-dog shuddered but would not budge an inch.

42

"Naughty Bart!" She slipped off to the floor. "I'll make him come," she said.

"If it's the same to you," said Vic, rather hastily, "I'd just as soon he stayed where he is."

"He's got to do what I want," she answered. She shook a tiny forefinger at him. "Bart, you just come here!"

The dog turned his blazing eyes on her and replied with a growl that shook his sides.

"Stop!" she ordered, and struck him sharply on the nose. He blinked and lowered his head under the blow, but though the snarling stopped his teeth flashed. She caught him by both jowls and tugged him forward.

"Let him be!" urged Vic.

"He's got to come!"

And come he did, step by halting step, while she hauled him, and now the snarling hoarse intakes of breath filled the room. Once she moved a little to one side and Vic caught the glint of two eyes, red-stained, which were fixed undeviatingly upon her face. Mixed with Vic's alarm at the great fighting beast was a peculiar uneasiness, for there was something uncanny in the determination, the fearlessness of this infant. When she stepped away the wolf-dog stood trembling visibly but his eyes were still not upon the man he hated or feared to approach but upon the child's face.

"Can you pat him now?" she asked, not for an instant turning to Gregg.

"No, but it's close enough," he assured her. "I don't want him any closer."

"He's got to come." She stamped. "Bart, you come here!"

He flinched forward, an inch. "Bart!" Her hands were clenched and her little body quivered with resolution; the snake-like head came to the very edge of the bed.

"Now pat him!" she commanded.

By very unpleasant degrees, Vic stretched his hand towards that growling menace.

"He'll take my arm off," he complained. Shame kept him from utterly refusing the risk.

"He won't bite you one bit," declared the child. "But

43

I'll hold his nose if you're afraid." And instantly she clasped the pointed muzzle between her hands.

Even when Vic's hand hovered above his head Bart had no eye for him, could not divert his gaze from the face of the child. Once, twice and again, delicately as one might handle bubbles, Gregg touched that scarred forehead.

"I made him come, didn't I?" she cried in triumph, and turned a tense little face towards Vic, but the instant her eyes moved the wolf-dog leaped away half the width of the room, and stood shivering, more devilish than ever. She stamped again.

"Bad, bad, *bad* Bart," she said angrily. "Shall I make him come again?"

"Leave him be," muttered Vic, closing his eyes. "Leave him be where he is, *I* don't want him."

"Oh," she said, "it's hard to make him do things, sometimes. But Daddy Dan can make him do *anything!*"

"Humph!" grunted Vic. He was remembering how at the master's order, Bart had crouched at his feet in the wood, an unchained murderer hungrily waiting for an excuse to kill. There was something very odd about the people of this house; and it would be a long time before he rid himself of the impression of the cold, steady eyes which had flashed up to him a moment before out of that baby face.

"Joan!" called a voice from beyond, and the soft fiber of it made Vic certain that it belonged to the rider of the black stallion. The little girl ran a step towards the door, and then stopped and shrank back against the bed.

If you're afraid your Dad'll find you here," said Vic, "just you run along."

She was nervously twisting her hands in her dress.

"Daddy Dan'll know," she whispered without turning. "And—and—he won't let me be afraid—even of him!"

A small hand slipped up, fumbled a bit, found the thumb of Vic Gregg, and closed softly over it. With this to steady her, she waited, facing the door.

CHAPTER VIII

Discipline

A light step crossed the outer room with something peculiar in its lightness, as if the heel were not touching the floor, with the effect of the padded fall of the feet of some great cat; there was both softness and the sense of weight. First, the wolf-dog pricked his ears and turned towards the door, the pudgy fist closed convulsively over Vic's thumb, and then his rescuer stood in the entrance.

"Hello, partner," called Vic. "I got company, you see. The door blew open and I asked your little girl in."

"I told you not to come here," said the other. Vic felt the child tremble, but there was no burst of excuses.

"She didn't want to come," he urged. "But I kep' on askin' her."

The emotionless eye of "Daddy Dan" held upon Joan. "I told you not to come," he said. Joan swallowed in mute agony, and the wolf-dog slipped to the side of the master and licked his hand as though in dumb intercession. The blood ran coldly in the veins of Gregg, as if he saw a fist raised to strike the little girl.

"You go out."

She went swiftly, at that, sidled past her father with her eyes lifted, fascinated, and so out the door where she paused an instant to flash back a wistful appeal. Nothing but silence, and then her feet pattering off into the outer room.

"Maybe you better go keep her company, Bart," said the father, and at this sign of relenting Vic felt his tensed muscles relaxing; the wolf whined softly and glided through the door.

"You feeling better?"

"Like a hoss off green feed. I been lyin' here drinkin' up the sunshine."

The other stood beside the open window and there he canted his head, his glance far off and intent.

"D'you hear?" he asked, turning sharply.

There was a fierce eagerness in his face.

"Hear what?"

"It's spring," he murmured, without answering more directly than this, and Vic felt that the other had changed again, grown understandable. Nevertheless, the shock of that sudden alteration at the window kept him watching his host with breathless interest. Whatever it was that the strange fellow heard, a light had gleamed in his eyes for a moment. As he sauntered back towards the bed just a trace of it lingered about him, a hint of sternness.

"Spring?" answered Gregg. "Yep, I smelled spring a few days back and I started out to find some action. You can see for yourself that I found it, partner." He stirred, uneasily, but it was necessary that the story should be told lest it reach the ears of this man from another source. It was one thing to shelter a fugitive from justice whose crime was unknown, perhaps trifling, but it might be quite another story if this gentle, singular man learned that his guest was a new-made murderer. Better that he should learn the tale now and form his prejudices in favor of Gregg. "I'll tell you the whole story," he began.

But the other shrugged his shoulders.

"You leave the story be," he said, and there was something in the quiet firmness of his manner which made it impossible for Vic to continue. "You're here and you're hurt and you need a pile of rest. That's about enough story for me."

Vic put himself swiftly in the place of the other. Suppose that he and Betty Neal should have a cabin off in the mountains like this, how would they receive a wounded fugitive from justice? As unquestioningly as this? In a surge of gratitude he looked mistily towards his host.

"Stranger," he said, "you're white. Damned white. That's all. My name's Vic Gregg and I come from——"

"Thanks," cut in the other. "I'm glad to know your name but in case anybody might be askin' me I wouldn't

46

care to know where you come from." He smiled. "I'm Dan Barry."

It had to be a left-handed shake on the part of Vic, a thing of which he often thought in the days that followed, but now he sent his memory hunting.

"Seems like I've heard your name before," he murmured. "I dunno where. Were you ever around Alder, Barry?"

"No." His manner suggested that the topic might as well be closed. He reached over and dropped his hand lightly on the forehead of Vic. A tingling current flowed from it into the brain of the wounded man. "Your blood's still a bit hot," he added. "Lie quiet and don't even think. You're safe here. They ain't a thing goin' to get at you. Not a thing. You'll stay till you get ready to leave. S'long. I'll see that you get something to eat."

He went out with that unusual, padding step which Vic had noticed before and closed the door softly behind him. In spite of that barrier Gregg could hear the noises from the next room quite clearly, as some one brought in wood and dropped it on a stone hearth, rattling. He fell into a pleasant doze, just stretching his body now and then to enjoy the coolness of the sheets, the delicious sense of being cared for and the returning strength in his muscles. Through that haze he heard voices, presently, which called him back in wakefulness.

"That ought to be good for him. Take it in, Kate."

"I shall. Dan, what has Joan done?"

"She went in there. I told her to leave him alone."

"But she says he asked her to come in—said he would take the blame."

"I told her not to go."

"Poor baby! She's outside, now, weeping her eyes out on Bart's shoulder and he's trying to comfort her."

It was purer English than Vic was accustomed to hear even from his schoolmistress, but more than the words, the voice surprised him, the low, controlled voice of a woman of gentle blood. He turned his head and looked out the window, baffled. Far above, shooting out of sight, went the slope of a mountain, a cliff shining in the slant sun of the afternoon here, a tumbled slide of rocks and débris

47

there, and over the shoulder of this mountain he saw white-headed monsters stepping back in range beyond range. Why should a girl of refinement choose the isolation of such a place as this for her home? It was not the only strange thing about this household, however, and he would dismiss conjectures until he was once more on his feet.

She was saying: "Won't you speak to her now?"

A little pause. Then: "No, not until evenin'."

"Please, Dan."

"She's got to learn."

A little exclamation of unhappiness and then the door moved open; Vic found himself looking up to the face with the golden hair which he remembered out of his nightmare. She nodded to him cheerily.

"I'm so happy that you're better," she said. "Dan says that the fever is nearly gone." She rested a large tray she carried on the foot of the bed and Vic discovered, to his great content, that it was not hard to meet her eyes. Usually girls embarrassed him, but he recognized so much of Joan in the features of the mother that he felt well acquainted at once. Motherhood, surely, sat as lightly on her shoulders as fatherhood did on Dan Barry, yet he felt a great pity as he looked at her, this flowerlike beauty lost in the rocks and snow with only one man near her. She was like music played without an audience except senseless things.

"Yep, I'm a lot better," he answered, "but it sure makes me terrible sorry, ma'am, that I got your little girl in trouble. Mostly, it was my fault."

She waved away all need of apology.

"Don't think an instant about that Mr. Gregg. Joan needs a great deal of disciplining." She laughed a little. "She has so much of her father in her, you see. Now, are you strong enough to lift yourself higher in the pillows?"

They managed it between them, for he was weaker than he thought and when he was padded into position with cushions she laid the tray across his knees. His head swam at sight of it. Forty-eight hours of fasting had sharpened his appetite, and the loaded tray whetted a razor edge, for a great bowl of broth steamed forth an exquisite fragrance on one side and beside it she lifted a napkin to let him peek at a slice of venison steak. Then there was butter, yellow as the gold for which he had been digging all winter, and real cream for his coffee—a whole pitcher of it—and snowy bread. Best of all, she did not stay to embarrass him with her watching while he ate, since above all things in the world a hungry man hates observation when the board is spread.

Afterwards, consuming sleep rippled over him from his feet to his eyes to his brain. He partially roused when the tray was removed, and the pillows slipped from under his back, but with a vague understanding that expert hands were setting the bed in order his senses fled once more.

Hours and hours later he opened his eyes in utter darkness with a thin, sweet voice still ringing in his ears. He could not place himself until he turned his head and saw a meager, broken, rectangular line of light which was the door, and immediately afterwards the voice cried: "Oh, Daddy Dan! And what did the wolf do then?"

"I'm comin' to that, Joan, but don't you talk about wolves so loud or old Black Bart'll think you're talkin' about him. See him lookin' at you now?"

"But please go on. I won't say one little word."

The man's voice began again, softly, so that not a word was audible to Gregg; he heard the crackle of burning logs upon the hearth; saw the rectangle of light flicker; caught a faint scent of wood smoke; and then he slept once more.

CHAPTER IX

The Long Arm of the Law

From the first the wound healed rapidly, for Vic's blood was perfectly pure, the mountain air a tonic which strengthened him, and his food and care of the best. The high-powered rifle bullet whipped cleanly through his shoulder, breaking no bone and tearing no ligament, and the flesh closed swiftly. Even Vic's mind carried no burden to oppress him in care for the future or regret for the past, for if he occasionally remembered the limp body of Hansen on the floor of Captain Lorrimer's saloon he could shrug the picture into oblivion. It had been fair fight, man to man, with all the odds in favor of Blondy, who had been allowed to pull his gun first. If Vic thought about the future at all, it was with a blind confidence that some time and in some unrevealed way he would get back to Alder and marry Betty Neal. In the meantime, as the days of the spring went mildly by, he was up and about and very soon there was only a little stiffness in his right arm to remind him of Pete Glass and the dusty roan.

He spent most of his time close to the cabin, for though he had forgotten the world there was no decisive proof that the world would forget him half so easily; that was not the way of the sheriff. He had been known to spend years in the hunt for a single misdoer and Vic had no care to wander out where he might be seen. Besides, it was very pleasant about the cabin. The house itself was built solidly, roomily, out of logs hewn on the timbered slopes above and dragged down to this little plateau. Three mountains, to the north, south and west, rolled back and up, cutting away the sunlight in the early afternoon, but at

50

this point the quick slopes put out shoulders and made, among them, a comfortable bit of rolling ground, deep soiled and fertile. Here, so Kate Barry assured him, the wild flowers came even earlier than they did in the valley so far below them, and to be sure when Vic first walked from the house he found the meadow aflame with color except for the space covered by the truck-garden and the corral. In that enclosure he found Grey Molly fenced away from the black with several other horses of commoner blood, for the stallion, he learned, recognized no fraternity of horseflesh, but killed what he could reach. Grey Molly was quite recovered from her long run, and she greeted him in her familiar way, with ears flattened viciously.

He might have stayed on here quite happily for any space of time, but more and more Vic felt that he was an intruder; he sensed it, rather than received a hint of word or eye. In the first place the three were complete in themselves, a triangle of happiness without need of another member for variety or interest. It was plain at a glance that the girl was whole-heartedly happy, and whatever incongruity lay between her and these rough mountains he began to understand that her love for Barry and the child made ample amends. As for the other two, he always thought of them in the same instant, for if the child had her eyes and her hair from her mother, she had her nature from the man. They were together constantly, on walks up the mountain, when she rode Black Bart up the steep places: in dips into the valley, when he carried her before him on the stallion. She had the same soft voice, the same quick furtive ways, the same soundless laughter, at times; and when Barry sat in the evening, as he often did for hours, staring at empty air, she would climb on his knee, place his unresisting arm around her, and lie looking up into his face, sharing his silences. Sometimes Vic wondered if the young mother were not troubled, made a little jealous by this perfect companionship, but he never found a trace of it. It was she, finally, who made him determine to leave as soon as his shoulder muscles moved with perfect freedom, for as the days slipped past he felt that she grew more and

51

more uneasy, and her eyes had a way of going from him to her husband as though she believed their guest a constant danger to Barry. Indeed, to some small extent he *was* a danger, for the law might deal hardly with a man who took a fugitive out of the very grip of its hand.

By a rather ironical chance, on the very morning when he decided that he must start his journey the next day but one, Vic learned that he must not linger even so long as that. Pete Glass and the law had not forgotten him, indeed, nearly so well as he had forgotten the law and Pete Glass, for as he sat in his room filling a pipe after breakfast the voice of Barry called him out, and he found his host among the rocks which rimmed the southern end of the plateau, in front of the house. To the north the ground fell away smoothly, rolled down to the side of the mountain, and then dipped easily to the valley—the only direction from which the cabin was accessible, though here the grade was possible for a buckboard. To the south the plateau ended in a drop that angled sharply down, almost a cliff in places, and from this point of vantage the eye carried nameless miles down the river.

"Are them friends of yours?" asked Dan Barry, as he stood among those rocks. "Take a long look." And he handed a strong pair of field glasses to Gregg.

The latter peered over the dizzy edge. Down there, in the very act of fording the river to get to their side of it, he marked five horsemen—no, six, for he almost missed the leader of the troop, a dusty figure which melted into the background. All the terror of the first flight rushed back on Vic. He stood palsied, not in fear of that posse but at the very thought of pursuit.

"There's only one way," he stammered at length. "I'll—Dan, give me a hand to get a saddle on Grey Molly and I'll laugh at 'em yet. Damn 'em!"

"What you goin' to do?" It was the same unhurried voice which had spoken to Vic on the day of the rescue and it irritated him in the same manner now. Kate had come running from the house with her apron fluttering.

"I'm going down that slope to the north," said Vic, "and I'll get by 'em hell-bent-for-election. Once I show my heels to that lot they're done!"

52

He talked as much to restore his courage as from confidence, for if the posse sighted him going down that slope on the gray it would take a super-horseman and a super-horse to escape before they closed the gap. Barry considered the situation with a new gleam in his eye.

"Wait a minute," he said, as Vic started towards the corral. "That way you got planned is a good way—to die. You listen to me."

But here Kate broke in on them. "Dan, what are you going to do?"

"I'm going to take the gray and go down the slope. I'm going to lead 'em off Vic's trail," said Barry quietly, but it seemed to Vic that he avoided his wife's eye.

The voice of Betty Neal, Vic knew, would have risen shrill at a time like this. Kate spoke even more low than usual, but there was a thing in her voice that struck a tremor through Gregg. "If it's death for him, what is it for you?"

"Nothing at all. If they see me and head for me before the way's clear, I'll let 'em come up and see they have the wrong man. If I get the chance, I'll lead 'em away. And Vic, you'll hit between those two mountains—see 'em?—and cut across country. No hoss could carry you there, except Satan, and you couldn't ride him. You'll have to go on foot but they'll never look for you on that side. When you get to the easy-goin', down in the valley, buy a hoss and hit for the railroad."

Kate turned on Vic, trembling. "Are you going to let him do it?" she asked. "Are you going to let him do it again?"

He had seen a certain promise of escape held before him the moment before, but pride made him throw that certainty away.

"Not in a million years," he answered. "I——"

"You'll do what I say, and you'll start now. I got a better idea than that. If you head just over the side of that north mountain you'll find a path that a hoss can follow. It won't take you clear away from them down below, but there ain't a chance in ten that they'll come that way. Take my old brown hoss with the white face. He'll carry you safe."

Vic hesitated. The fierce eyes of Kate were on him and with all his soul he wanted to play the man, but liberty was sweet, sweeter than ever to Vic. She seemed to give him up as he stood there with his heart in his throat; she turned back to Barry.

"Dan!" she pleaded.

She had not touched him, but he made a vague gesture as though brushing away a restraining hand. She cried: "If you come close to them—if they start shooting —you might want to fight back——"

"They shot before," he answered, "and I didn't fire once."

"But the second time?"

To be sure, there would be danger in it, but as Barry himself had said, if the way was closed to him he could surrender to them, and they could not harm him. Vic tried in vain to understand this overmastering terror in the girl, for she seemed more afraid of what Dan might do to the posse than what the posse might do to Dan.

"This ain't a day for fightin'," said Dan, and he waved towards the mountains. It was one of those misty spring days when the sun raises a vapor from the earth and the clouds blow low around the upper peaks; every ravine was poured full of blue shadow, and even high up the slopes, where patches of snow had melted, grass glimmered, a tender green among the white. "This ain't a day for fightin'," he repeated.

A shrill, quavering neigh, like the whinny of a galloping horse, rang from beyond the house, and Vic saw the black stallion racing up and down his corral. Back and forth he wove, then raced straight for the bars, flashed above them, and stood free beyond, with the sunshine trembling on him. He seemed to pause, wondering what to do with his new freedom, then he came at a loose gallop for the master. Not Satan alone, for now Black Bart slid across the plateau like a shadow, weaving among the boulders, and came straight towards Barry. Vic himself felt a change, a sort of uneasy happiness; he breathed it with the air. The very sunlight was electric. He saw Kate run close to Barry.

"If you go this time, you'll never come back, Dan!"

The black stallion swung up beside them, and as he halted his hoofs knocked a rattling spray of pebbles ahead. On the other side of the woman and the man the wolf-dog ran uneasily here and there, trying to watch the face of the master which Kate obscured.

"I ain't goin' far. I just want to get a hoss runnin' under me enough to cut a wind."

"Even Satan and Bart feel what I feel. They came without being called. They never do that unless there's danger ahead. What can I do to convince you? Dan, you'll drive me mad!"

He made no answer, and if the girl wished him to stay now seemed the time for persuasion; but she gave up the argument suddenly. She turned away, and Vic saw in her face the same desperate, helpless look as that of a boy who cannot swim, beyond his depth in the river. There was no sign of tears; they might come afterwards.

What had come over them? This desperation in Kate, this touch of anxiety in the very horse and the wolf-dog? Vic forgot his own danger while he stared and it seemed to him that the spark of change had come from Barry. There was something in his eyes which Vic found hard to meet.

"The moment you came I knew you brought bad luck with you!" cried Kate. "He brought you in bleeding. He saved you and came in with blood on his hands and I guessed at the end. Oh, I wish you——"

"Kate!" broke in Barry.

She dropped upon one of the stones and buried her face in her hands and Dan paid no more attention to her.

"Hurry up" he said. "They're across the river."

And Vic gave up the struggle, for the tears of Kate made him think of Betty Neal and he followed Dan towards the corral. Around them the stallion ran like a hunting dog eager to be off.

CHAPTER X

One Trail Ends

"You can trust Grey Molly to me, Vic," said Dan, standing at the head of the gray mare. "I'll keep her as safe as if she was Satan.

Gregg watched her almost sadly. He had always taken a rather childish pride in her fierceness. She knew him as a dog knows its master and he had always been the only one who could handle her readily in the saddle. But one who knew nothing of horses and their ways could see the entente which had been instantly established between Barry and Grey Molly. When he spoke her ears pricked. When he raised his hand she stretched her nose inquisitively.

There was no pitch in her when Barry swung into the saddle and that was a thing without precedent in Molly's history. She tried none of her usual catlike side-steps and throwing of the head. Altogether, Vic was troubled even as he would have been at the sight of Betty Neal in the arms of another man. It was desertion.

"Dan," he said, "I know what you've done for me and I know what you're doin' now." He took the slender hand of the other in his big paw. "If the time comes when I can pay you back, so help me God——"

"Oaths don't do no good," cut in Barry without a trace of emotion. He added frankly: "It ain't altogether for your sake. Those gents down there have played tag once with me and now I'd like to play with them. Molly's fresh to-day."

He was already looking over his shoulder while he spoke; as if his mind were even then at work upon the posse.

56

"S'long."

"S'long, partner. Good-luck."

So they parted and Vic, jogging slowly up the steep path, saw Grey Molly wheeled and sent at a sweeping gallop over the meadow. His heart leaped jealously—and the next moment went out in a flood of gratitude, admiration, as Barry swung off the shoulder of the mountain, waved his hat towards Kate, and dipped at once out of sight.

The shelving ground along which Barry rode sometimes was a broad surface like a spacious, graded road; again it shelved away and opened a view of all the valley. When he reached the first of these places the rider looked back and down and saw the posse skirting rapidly on his side of the river, behind him and close to the cliff. They rode at an easy lope, and he could see that their heads were bent to watch the ground. Even at this casual gait they would reach the point at which he and the gray must swing onto the floor of the valley before him unless he urged Molly to top speed. He must get there at a sufficient distance from them to escape close rifle fire, and certainly beyond point-blank revolver range. Accordingly he threw his weight more into the stirrups and over the withers of the mare. This brought greater poundage on her forehand and made her apt to stumble or actually miss her step, but it increased her running power.

There was no need of a touch of the spurs. The gathering of the reins seemed to tell Molly everything. One ear flickered back, then she leaped out at full speed. It was as though the mind of the man had sent an electric current down the reins and told her his thought. Now she floundered at her foot, struck a loose stone, now she veered sharply and wide to escape a boulder, now she cleared a gulley with a long leap, and riding high as he was, bent forward out of balance to escape observation from below. It was only a miracle of horsemanship that kept her from breaking her neck as they lurched down the pitch. Grey Molly seemed to be carrying no weight, only a clinging intelligence.

At this speed he was sure to reach the valley safely in front unless the posse caught sight of him on the way and gave chase, and Barry counted on that instinct in hunting men which makes them keep their eyes low—the same sense which leads a searcher to look first under the bed and last of all at the wall and ceiling. Once more, as he neared his goal, he looked back and down, and there came the six horsemen, their quirts swinging, their hat-brims blown straight up as they raced at full speed. They had seen the gray and they rode for blood.

The outstretched neck of Grey Molly, her flattened ears, the rapid clangor of her hoofs on the rocks, seemed to indicate that she already was doing her uttermost, but after the glimpse of the pursuit, Barry crouched a little lower, his hand gathering the reins just behind her head, his voice was near her, speaking softly, quickly. She responded with a snort of effort, as though she realized the danger and willingly accepted it. One ear, as she rushed down the slope, was pricked and one flagged back to the guiding, strengthening voice of the rider.

The path wound in leisurely curves now, but there was a straight cut down a slide of gravel, a dangerous slope even in firm ground, a terrible angle with those loose pebbles underfoot. Yet this was a time for chance-taking. Already the dusty man on the roan rode with his revolver balanced for the snap shot. The next instant his gun swung down, he actually reined up in astonishment. The fugitive had flung himself far back against the cantle and sent Grey Molly at the slide. It was not a matter of running as the mare shot over the brink. Molly sat back on her haunches, braced her forelegs, and went down like an avalanche. Over the rush and roar of the pebbles, over the yell of wonder from the pursuers, she heard the voice of her rider, a clear and steady voice, and the tautened reins telegraphed to her bewildered mind the wish of the man. She struck the level with stunning force, toppled, nearly fell, and then straightened along her course in a staggering gallop. Started from its nice balance by the rush of stones they loosened, a ten-ton rock came toppling after, leaped up from the valley floor like a live thing, and then thundered away towards the river.

Grey Molly, finding her legs once more, tried the level going. She had beaten the same horses before under

58

the crushing impost of Gregg's weight. With this lighter rider who clung like a part of her, who gave perfectly to the rhythm of her gallop, she fairly walked away from the posse. Once, twice and again the gun spoke from the hand of Pete Glass, but it was the taking of a long last chance rather than a sign of closing on his chase. In ten minutes Grey Molly dipped out of sight among the hills.

After the first hour Barry could have cut away across country with little fear of discovery from the sheriff, but he was in no hurry to escape. Sometimes he dismounted and looked to his cinches and talked to the horse. Grey Molly listened with pricking ears and often canted her head to one side as though she strove to understand the game.

It was a new and singular pleasure to Barry. He was accustomed to the exhaustless, elastic strength of Satan, with the cunning brain of a beast of prey and the speed of an antelope. On the black horse he could have ridden circles around that posse all day. But Grey Molly was a different problem. She was not a force to be simply directed and controlled. She was something to be helped. Her very weakness, compared with the stallion, appealed to him. And it was a thrilling pleasure to feel his power over her grow until she, also, seemed to have entered the game.

A game it was, as he had said to Vic when they parted, with the rather essential difference that in this pastime one was tagged with a forty-five caliber chunk of lead and was quite apt to remain "it" for the remainder of eternity. Barry dropped further and further back towards the posse. The danger fascinated him. Once he whistled high and shrill as a hawk's scream from the top of a bluff while the posse labored through a ravine below. He saw the guns flash out, and waited. He heard the sing of the bullets around him, and the splashing lead on a solid-rock-face just beneath him; he listened till the deep echoes spoke from the gulch, then waved his hat and disappeared.

This was almost defeating the purpose of his play, for if he came that close again they would probably make out that they were following a decoy. Accordingly, since he had now drawn them well away from Vic's line of escape, he turned his back reluctantly on the posse and struck across the hills.

He kept on for the better part of an hour before he doubled and swung in a wide circle towards his cabin. He had laid out a course which the wise sheriff could follow until dark and be none the wiser; and if Pete Glass were the finest trailer who ever studied sign and would never be able to read the tokens of the return ride. Accordingly, with all this well in mind, he brought Grey Molly to a full halt and grazed around utterly stunned by surprise, when, half way up the valley, a rifle spoke small but sharp from one side, and a bullet clipped the rocks not the length of the horse away. He understood. When he cut straightaway across the country he had indeed left a baffling trail, a trail so dim, in fact, that Pete Glass had wisely given it up and taken the long chance by cutting back to the point at which the hunt began. So their paths crossed. Barry spoke sharply to the mare and loosed the reins, but she started into a full gallop too late. There came a brief hum, a thudding blow, and Grey Molly pitched forward.

CHAPTER XI

A New Trail Begins

If he had been an ordinary rider, sitting heavily far back in the saddle, at the end of a long ride, Barry would either have been flung clear and smashed horribly against the rocks, or, more likely, he would have been entangled in the stirrups and crushed to death instantly by the weight of his horse; but he rode always lightly poised and when the mare pitched forward his feet were already clear of the stirrups. He landed, catlike, on hands and feet, unhurt.

It had been a long shot, a lucky hit even for a marksman of the sheriff's caliber, and now the six horsemen streamed over a distant hilltop and swept into the valley to take their quarry dead, or half dead, from his fall. However, that approaching danger was nothing in the eye of Barry. He ran to the fallen mare and caught her head in his arms. She ceased her struggles to rise as soon as he touched her and whinneyed softly. The left foreleg lay twisted horribly beneath her, broken. Grey Molly had run her last race, and as Barry kneeled, holding the brave head close to him, he groaned, and looked away from her eyes. It was only an instant of weakness, and when he turned to her again he was drawing his gun from its holster.

The beating hoofs of the posse as they raced towards him made a growing murmur through the clear air. Barry glanced towards them with a consummate loathing. They had killed a horse to stop a man, and to him it was more than murder. What harm had she done them except to carry her rider bravely and well? The tears of rage and sorrow which a child sheds welled into the eyes of Dan Barry. Every one of them had a hand in this horrible killing; every one of them was, to that half animal and half childish nature, a murderer.

His chin was on his shoulder; the quiver of pain in her nostrils ended as he spoke; and while the fingers of his left hand trailed caressingly across her forehead, his right carried the muzzle to her temple.

"Brave Molly, good girl," he whispered, "they'll pay for you a death for a death and a man for a hoss." The yellow which had glinted in his eyes during the run was afire now. "It ain't far; only a step to go; and then you'll be where they ain't any saddles, nor any spurs to gall you, Molly, but just pastures that's green all year, and nothin' to do but loaf in the sun and smell the wind. Here's good luck to you, girl."

His gun spoke sharp and short and he laid the limp head reverently on the ground.

It had all happened in very few seconds, and the posse was riding through the river, still a long shot off, when Barry drew his rifle from its case on the saddle. Moreover, the failing light which had made the sheriff's hit so much a matter of luck was now still dimmer, yet Barry snapped his gun to the shoulder and fired the instant the butt lay in the grove. For another moment nothing changed in the appearance of the riders, then a man leaned out of his saddle and fell full length in the water.

Around him his companions floundered, lifted and placed him on the bank, and then threw themselves from their horses to take shelter behind the first rocks they could find; they had no wish to take chances with a man who could snap-shoot like this in such a light, at such a distance. By the time they were in position their quarry had slipped out of sight and they had only the blackening boulders for targets.

"God A'mighty," cried Ronicky Joe, "are you goin' to let that murderin' hound-dog get clear off, Pete? Boys, who's with me for a run at him?"

For it was Harry Fisher who had fallen and lay now on the wet bank with his arms flung wide and a red spot rimmed with purple in the center of his forehead; and Fisher was Ronicky Joe's partner.

"You lay where you are," commanded the sheriff, and

indeed there had been no rousing response to Ronicky Joe's appeal.

"You yaller quitters," groaned Joe. "Give me a square chance and I'll tackle Vic Gregg alone day or night, on hoss or on foot. Are we five goin' to lay down to him?"

"If that was Vic Gregg," answered the sheriff, slipping over the insult with perfect calm, "I wouldn't of told you to scatter for cover; but that ain't Vic."

"Pete, what in hell are you drivin' at?"

"I say it ain't Vic," said the sheriff. "Vic is a good man with a hoss and a good man with a gun, but he couldn't never ride like the gent over there in the rocks, and he couldn't shoot like him."

He pointed, in confirmation, at the body of Harry Fisher.

"You can rush that hill if you want, but speakin' personal, I ain't ready to die."

A thoughtful silence held the others until Silver Waldron broke it with his deep bass. "You ain't far off, Pete. I done some thinkin' along them lines when I seen him standin' up there over the arroyo wavin' his hat at the bullets. Vic didn't never have the guts for that."

All the lower valley was gray, dark in comparison with the bright peaks above it, before the sheriff rose from his place and led the posse towards the body of Grey Molly. There they found as much confirmation of Pete's theory as they needed, for Vic's silver-mounted saddle was known to all of them, and this was a plain affair which they found on the dead horse. Waldron pushed back his hat to scratch his head. "Look at them eyes, boys," he suggested. "Molly has been beatin' us all day and she looks like she's fightin' us still."

The sheriff was not a man of very many words, and surely of little sentiment; perhaps it was the heat of the long chase which now made him take off his hat so that the air could reach his sweaty forehead. "Gents," he said, "she lived game and she died game. But they ain't no use of wastin' that saddle. Take it off."

And that was Grey Molly's epitaph.

They decided to head straight back for the nearest town with the body of Harry Fisher, and, fagged by the desperate riding of that day, they let their horses go with loose rein, at a walk. Darkness gathered; the last light faded from even the highest peaks; the last tinge of color dropped out of the sky as they climbed from the valley. Now and then one of the horses cleared its nostrils with a snort, but on the whole they went in perfect silence with the short grass silencing the hoofbeats, and never a word passed from man to man.

Beyond doubt, if it had not been for that same silence, if it had not been for the slowness with which they drifted through the dark, what follows could never have happened. They had crossed a hill, and descended into a very narrow ravine which came to so sharp a point that the horses had to be strung out in single file. The ravine twisted to the right and then the last man of the procession heard the sheriff call: "Halt, there! Up with your hands, or I'll drill you!" When they swung from side to side, craning their heads to look, they made out a shadowy horseman facing Pete head on. Then the sheriff's voice again: "Gregg, I'm considerable glad to meet up with you."

If that meeting had taken place in any other spot probably Gregg would have taken his chance on escaping through the night, but in this narrow pass he could swing to neither side and before he could turn the brown horse entirely around the sheriff might pump him full of lead. They gathered in a solemn quiet around him; the irons were already upon his wrists.

"All right, boys," he said, "you've got me, but you'll have to give in that you had all the luck."

A moment after that sharp command in the familiar, dreaded voice of Pete Glass, Vic had been glad that the long flight was over. Eventually this was bound to come. He would go back and face the law, and three men lived to swear that Blondy had gone after his gun first.

"Maybe luck," said the sheriff. "How d' you come back this way?"

"Made a plumb circle," chuckled Gregg. "Rode like a fool not carin' where I hit out for, and the end of it was that it was dark before I'd had sense to watch where the sun went down."

"Kind of cheerful, ain't you?" cut in Ronicky Joe, and his voice was as dry as the crisping leaves in an autumn wind.

"They ain't any call for me to wear crêpe yet," answered Gregg. "Worst fool thing I ever done was to cut and run for it. The old Captain will tell you gents that Blondy went for his gun first—had it clean out of the leather before I touched mine."

He paused, and the silence of those dark figures sank in upon him.

"I got to warn you," said Pete Glass, "that what you say now can be used agin you later on before the jury."

"My God, boys," burst out Vic, "d' you think I'm a plain, low-down, murderin' snake? Harry, ain't you got a word for me? Are you like the rest of 'em?"

No voice answered.

"Harry," said Ronicky, "why don't you speak to him?"

It was a brutal thing to do, but Ronicky was never a gentle sort in his best moments; he scratched a match and held it so that under the spluttering light Gregg found himself staring into the face of Harry Fisher. And he could not turn his eyes away until the match burned down to Ronicky's finger tip and then dropped in a streak of red to the ground.

Then the sheriff spoke cold and hard.

"Partner," he said, "in the old days, maybe your line of talk would do some good, but not now. You picked that fight with Blondy. You knew you was faster on the draw and Hansen didn't have a chance. He was the worst shot in Alder and everybody in Alder knew it. You picked that fight and you killed your man, and—you're goin' to hang for it."

Another hush; no murmur of assent or dissent.

"But they's one way out for you, Gregg, and I'm layin' it clear. We wanted you bad, and we got you; but they's another man we want a lot worse. A pile! Gregg, take me where I can find the gent what done for Harry Fisher and you'll never stand up in front of a jury. You got my word on that."

CHAPTER XII

The Crisis

Those mountains above the Barry cabin were, as he told Vic Gregg, inaccessible to men on horseback except by one path, yet there was a single class of travelers who roamed at will through far more difficult ground than this. Speaking in general, where a man can go a burro can go, and where a burro can go he usually manages to carry his pack. He crawls up a raged down-pitch of rocks that comes dangerously close to the perpendicular; he walks securely along a crumbling ledge with half his body over a thousand yards of emptiness. Therefore the prospectors with their borros have combed the worst mountains of the West and it was hardly a surprise to Kate Barry when she saw two men come down the steepest slope above the cabin with two little pack animals scrambling and sliding before them. It was still some time before nightfall, but the sun had dropped out of sight fully an hour ago and now the western mountains were blackening against a sky whose thin, clear blue grew yellow towards evening.

Against that dark mass of the mountainside, she could not make out the two travelers clearly, so she shaded her eyes and peered up, high up. The slope was so sheer that if one of the four figures lost footing it would come crashing to her very feet. When they saw her and shouted down the sound fell as clearly as if they had called from the cabin, yet they had a good half hour's labor between that greeting and the moment they came out on the level before Kate. From the instant they called she remained in motionless, deep thought, and when they came now into full view, she cried out joyously: "Buck, oh Buck!" and ran towards them. Even the burros stopped and the men stood statue-like; it is rarely enough that one finds a human being in those mountains, almost an act of Providence that leads to a house, and a miracle when the trail crosses the path of a friend. The prospectors came out of their daze with a shout and rushed to meet her. Each of them had her by a hand, wringing it; they talked all together in a storm of words.

"Kate, I'm dreamin'!—Dear old Buck!—Have you forgotten me?—Lee Haines! I should say not.—Don't pay any attention to him. Five years. And I've been hungerin' to see you all that—.—Where have you been?—Everywhere! but this is the best thing I've seen.—Come in.—Wait till we get these packs off the poor little devils.—Oh, I'm so glad to see you; so glad!—Hurry up, Lee. Your fingers asleep?—How long have you been out?—Five months.—Then you're hungry.—We've just ate.—But a piece of pie?—Pie? I've been dreamin' of pie!"

A fire already burned in the big living-room of the cabin, for at this season, at such an altitude, the shadows were always cold, and around the fire they gathered, each of the men with half a huge pie before him. They were such as one might expect that mountain region to produce, big, gaunt, hard-muscled. They had gone unshaven for so long that their faces were clothed not with an unsightly stubble but with strong, short beard that gave them a certain grim dignity and made their eyes seem sunken. They were opposite types, which is usually the case when two men strike out together. Buck Daniels was black-haired, with an ugly, shrewd face and a suggestion of rather dangerous possibilities of swift action; but Lee Haines was a great bulk of a man, with tawny beard, handsome, in a leonine fashion, more poised than Daniels, fitted to crush. The sharp glance of Buck flitted here and there, in ten seconds he knew everything in the room; the steady blue eye of Lee Haines went leisurely from place to place and lingered; but both of them stared at Kate as if they could not have enough of her. They talked without pause while they ate. A stranger in the room would have sealed their lips in utter taciturnity, but here they sat

67

with a friend, five months of loneliness and labor behind them, and they gossiped like girls.

Into the jangle of talk cut a thin, small voice from outside, a burst of laughter. Then: "Bart, you *silly* dog!" and Joan stood at the open door with her hand buried in the mane of the wolf-dog. The fork of Buck Daniels stopped half-way to his lips and Lee Haines straightened until the chair groaned.

They spoke together, hushed voices: "Kate!"

"Come here, Joan!" Her face glistened with pride, and Joan came forward with wide eyes, tugging Black Bart along in a reluctant progress.

"It ain't possible!" whispered Buck Daniels. "Honey, come here and shake hands with your Uncle Buck." The gesture called forth deep throated warning from Bart, and he caught back his hands with a start.

"It's always that way," said Kate, half amused, half vexed; "Bart won't let a soul touch her when Dan isn't home. Good old Bart, go away, you foolish dog! Don't you see these are friends?"

He cringed a little under the shadow of the hand which waved him off but his only answer was a silent baring of the teeth.

"You see how it is. I'm almost afraid to touch her myself when Dan's away; she and Bart bully me all day long."

In the meantime the glance of Joan had cloyed itself with sufficient examination of the strangers, and now she turned back towards the door and the meadow beyond.

"Bart!" she called softly. The sharp ears of the dog quivered; he came to attention with a start. "Look! Get it for me!"

One loud scraping of his claws on the floor as he started, and Black Bart went like a bolt through the door with Joan scrambling after him, screaming with excitement; from the outside, they heard the cry of a frightened squirrel, and then its angry chattering from a place of safety up a tree.

"Shall I call her back again?" asked Kate.

"Not if Bart comes with her," answered Lee Haines. "I've seen enough of him to last me a while."

68

"Well, we'll have her to ourselves when Dan comes, of course Bart leaves her to tag around after Dan."

"When is he comin' back?" asked Buck, with polite interest.

"Anytime. I don't know. But he's always here before it's completely dark."

The glance of Buck Daniels kicked over to Lee Haines, exchanged meanings with him, and came back to Kate.

"Terrible sorry," he said, "but I s'pose we'll have to be on our way before it's plumb dark."

"Go so soon as that? Why, I won't let you."

"I——" began Haines, fumbling for words.

"We got to get down in the valley before it's dark," filled in Buck.

Suddenly she laughed, frankly, happily.

"I know what you mean, but Dan is changed; he isn't the same man he used to be."

"Yes?" queried Buck, without conviction.

"You'll have to see him to believe; Buck, he doesn't even whistle any more."

"What?"

"Only goes about singing, now."

The two men exchanged glances of such astonishment that Kate could not help but notice and flush a little.

"Well," murmured Buck, "Bart doesn't seem to have changed much from the old days."

She laughed slowly, letting her mind run back through such happiness as they could not understand and when she looked up she seemed to debate whether or not it would be worth while to let them in on the delightful secret. The moment she dwelt on the burning logs they gazed at her and then to each other with utter amazement as if they sat in the same room with the dead come to life. No care of motherhood had marked her face, but on the white, even forehead was a sign of peace; and drifting over her hands and on the white apron across her lap the firelight pooled dim gold, the wealth of contentment.

"If you'd been here to-day you would have seen how changed he is. We had a man with us whom Dan had taken while he was running from a posse, wounded, and kept him here until he was well, and——"

"That's Dan," murmured Lee Haines. "He's gold all through when a man's in trouble."

"Shut up, Lee," cut in Buck. He sat forward in his chair, drinking up her story. "Go on."

"This morning we saw the same posse skirting through the valley and knew that they were on the old trail. Dan sent Gregg over the hills and rode Vic's horse down so that the posse would mistake him, and he could lead them out of the way. I was afraid, terribly, I was afraid that if the posse got close and began shooting Dan would——"

She stopped; her eyes begged them to understand.

"Go on," said Lee Haines, shuddering slightly. "I know what you mean."

"But I watched him ride down the slope," she cried joyously, "and I saw the posse close on him—almost on top of him when he reached the valley. I saw the flash of their guns. I saw them shoot. I wasn't afraid that Dan would be hurt, for he seems to wear a charm against bullets—I wasn't much afraid of that, but I dreaded to see him turn and go back through that posse like a storm. But——" she caught both hands to her breast and her bright face tilted up—"even when the bullets must have been whistling around him he didn't look back. He rode straight on and on, out of view, and I knew"—her voice broke with emotion—"oh, Buck, I knew that he had won, and I had won; that he was safe forever; that there was no danger of him ever slipping back into that terrible other self; I knew that I'd never again have to dream of that whistling in the wind; I knew that he was ours—Joan's and mine——"

"By God," broke out Buck, "I'm happier than if you'd found a gold mine, Kate. It don't seem no ways possible —but if you seen that with your own eyes, it's true. He's changed."

"I've been almost afraid to be happy all these years," she said, "but now I want to sing and cry at the same time. My heart is so full that it's overflowing, Buck."

She brushed the tears away and smiled at them.

70

"Tell me all about yourselves. Everything. You first, Lee. You've been longer away."

He did not answer for a moment, but sat with his head fallen, watching her thoughtfully. Women had been the special curse in Lee Haines' life; they had driven him to the crime that sent him West into outlawry long years before; through women, as he himself foreboded, he would come at last to some sordid, petty end; but here sat the only one he had loved without question, without regret, purely and deeply, and as he watched her, more beautiful than she had been in her girlhood, it seemed, as he heard the fitful laughter of Joan outside, the old sorrow came storming up in him and the sense of loss.

"What have I been doing?" he murmured at length. He shrugged away his last thoughts. "I drifted about for a while after the pardon came down from the governor. People knew me, you see, and what they knew about me didn't please them. Even to-day Jim Silent and Jim Silent's crew isn't forgotten. Then—don't look at me like that, Kate; no, I played straight all the time—then I ran into Buck and he and I had tried each other out, we had at least one thing in common"—here he looked at Buck and they both flushed—"and we made a partnership of it. We've been together five years now."

"I knew you could break away, Lee. I used to tell you that."

"You helped me more than you knew," he said quietly.

She smiled and then turned to escape him. "And now you, Buck?"

"Since then we've made a bit of coin punching cows and we've blown it in again prospecting. Blown it in? Kate, we've shot enough powder to lift that mountain yonder but all we've got is color. You could gild the sky with what we've seen but we haven't washed enough dust to wear a hole in a tissue-paper pocket. I'll tell you the whole story. Lee packs a jinx with him. But—Haines, did you ever see a lion as big as that?"

The dimness of evening had grown rapidly through the room while they talked and now the light from the door was far less than the glow of the fire. The yellow flicker picked out a dozen pelts stretching as rugs on the floor

71

or hanging along the wall; that to which Buck pointed was an enormous skin of a mountain lion stretched sidewise, for if it had been hung straight up a considerable portion of the tail must have dragged on the floor. Buck went to examine it. Presently he exclaimed in surprise and he passed his fingers over it as though searching for something.

"Where was it shot, Kate? I don't find nothin' but this cut that looks like his knife slipped when he was skinnin'."

"It was a knife that killed it."

"What!"

"Don't ask me about it; I see the picture of it in my dreams still. The lion had dragged the trap into a cave and Bart followed it. Dan went in pushing his rifle before him, but when he tried to fire it jammed."

"Yes?" they cried together.

"Don't ask me the rest!"

They would hardly have let her off so easily if it had not been for the entrance of Joan who had come back on account of the darkness. Black Bart went promptly to a corner of the hearth and lay down with his head on his paws and the little girl sat beside him watching the fire, her head leaning wearily on his shoulder. Kate went to the door.

"It's almost night," she said. "Why isn't he here?" She started. "Buck, they couldn't have overtaken Dan?"

Buck Daniels grinned reassuringly.

"Not unless his hoss is a pile of bones; if it has any heart in it, Dan'll run away from anything on four legs. No call for worryin', Kate. He's simply led 'em a long ways off and waited for evenin' before he doubled back. He'll come back right enough. If they didn't catch him that first run they'll never get the wind of him."

It quieted her for a time, but as the minutes slipped away, as the darkness grew more and more heavy until a curtain of black fell across the open door, they could see that she was struggling to control her trouble, they could see her straining to catch some distant sound. Lee Haines began to talk valiantly, to beguile the waiting time, and Buck Daniels did his share with stories of their

72

prospecting, but eventually more and more often silences came on the group. They began to watch the fire and they winced when a log crackled, or when the sap in a green place hissed. By degrees they pushed farther and farther back so that the light would not strike so fully upon them, for in some way it became difficult to meet each other's eyes.

Only Joan was perfectly at ease. She played for a time with the ears of Black Bart, or pried open his mouth and made him show the great white fangs, or scratched odd designs on the hearth with pieces of charcoal; but finally she lost interest in all these things and let her head lie on the rough pelt of the wolf-dog, sound asleep. The firelight made her hair a patch of gold.

Black Bart slept soundly, too, that is, as soundly as one of his nature could sleep, for every now and then one of his ears twitched, or he stirred a paw, or an eyelid quivered up. Yet they all started when he jumped from his sleep into full wakefulness; the motion made Joan sit up, rubbing her eyes, and Black Bart reached the center of the room noiselessly. He stood facing the door, motionless.

"It's Dan," cried Kate. "Bart hears him! Good old Bart!"

The dog pointed up his nose, the hair about his neck bristled into a ruff, and out of his quaking body came a sound that seemed to moan and whimper from the distance at first, but drew nearer, louder, packed the room with terror, the long drawn howl of a wolf.

73

CHAPTER XIII

Equal Payment

They knew what it meant; even Joan had heard the cry of the lone wolf hunting in the lean time of winter, and of all things sad, all things lonely, all things demoniacal, the howl of a wolf stands alone. Lee Haines reached for his gun, little Joan stood up silent on the hearth, but Kate and Buck Daniels sat listening with a sort of hungry terror, as the cry sobbed away to quiet. Then out of the mountains and the night came an answer so thin, so eerie, one might have said it was the voice of the mountains and white stars grown audible; it stole on the ear as the pulse of a heart comes to the consciousness.

Truly it was an answer to the cry of the wolf-dog, for in the slender compass it carried the same wail, the same unearthy quality with this great difference, that a thrilling happiness went through it, as if some one walked through the mountains and rejoiced in the unknown terrors. A sob formed in the throat of Kate and the wolf turned its head and looked at her, and the yellow of things that see in the night swam in its eyes. Lee Haines struck the arm of Buck Daniels.

"Buck, let's get clear of this. Let's start. He's coming."

At the whisper Buck turned a livid face; one could see him gather his strength.

"I stick," he said with difficulty, as though his lips were numb. "She'll need me now."

Lee Haines stood in a moment's indecision but then settled back in his chair and gripped his hands together. They both sat watching the door as if the darkness were a magnet of inescapable horror. Only Joan, of all in that room, showed no fear after the first moment. Her face was blanched indeed, but she tilted it up now, smiling; she stole towards the door, but Kate caught the child and gathered her close with strangling force. Joan made no attempt to escape.

"S—sh!" she cautioned, and raised a plump little forefinger. "Munner, don't you hear? Don't you like it?"

As if the sound had turned a corner, it broke all at once clearly over them in a rain of music; a man's whistling. It went out; it flooded about them again like beautiful, cold light. Once again it stopped, and now they sensed, rather than heard, a light, rapid, paddling step that approached the cabin. Dan Barry stood in the door and in that shadowy place his eyes seemed luminous. He no longer whistled, but a spirit went from him which carried the same sense of the untamed, the wild happiness which died out with his smile as he looked around the room. The brim of his hat curved up, his neckerchief seemed to flutter a little. The wolf-dog reached the threshold in the same instant and stood looking steadily up into the face of the master.

"Daddy Dan!" cried Joan.

She had slipped from the nerveless arms of Kate and now ran towards her father, but here she faltered, there she stopped with her arms slowly falling back to her sides. He did not seem to see her, but looked past her, far beyond every one in the room as he walked to the wall and took down a bridle that hung on a peg. Kate laid her hands on the arms of the chair, but after the first effort to rise, her strength failed.

"Dan!" she said. It was only a whisper, a heartstopping sound. "Dan!" Her voice rang, then her arms gathered to her, blindly, Joan, who had shrunk back. "What's happened?"

"Molly died."

"Died."

"They broke her leg."

"The posse!"

"With a long shot."

"What are you going to do!"

"Get Satan. Go for a ride."

"Where?"

75

He looked about him, troubled, and then frowned.

"I dunno. Out yonder."

He waved his arm. Black Bart followed the turn of the master's body, and switching around in front continued to stare up into Dan's face.

"You're going back after the posse!"

"No, I'm done with them."

"What do you mean?"

"They paid for Grey Molly."

"You shot one of their—horses?"

"A man."

"God help us!" Then life came to her; she sprang up and ran between him and the door. "You shan't go. If you love me!" She was only inches from Black Bart, and the big animal showed his teeth in silent hate.

"Kate, I'm goin'. Don't stand in the door."

Joan, slipping around Bart, stood clinging to the skirts of her mother and watched the face of Dan, fascinated, silent.

"Tell me where you're going. Tell me when you're coming back. Dan, for pity!"

Loud as a trumpet, a horse neighed from the corral. Dan had stood with an uncertain face, but now he smiled.

"D'you hear? I got to go!"

"I heard Satan whinny. But what does that mean? How does that make you go?"

"Somewhere," he murmured, "something's happening. I felt it on the wind when I was comin' up the pass."

"If you—oh, Dan, you're breaking my heart!"

"Stand out of the door."

"Wait till the morning."

"Don't you see I can't wait?"

"One hour, ten minutes. Buck—Lee Haines——"

She could not finish, but Buck Daniels stepped closer, trying to make a smile grow on his ashen face.

"Another minute, Dan, and I'll tell a man you've forgotten me."

Barry pivoted suddenly as though uneasy at finding something behind him, and Daniels winced.

"Hello, Buck. Didn't see you was here. Lee Haines? Lee, this is fine."

He passed from one to the other and his handshake was only the elusive passage of his fingers through their palms. Haines shrugged his shoulders to get rid of a weight that clung to him; a touch of color came back to his face.

"Look here, Dan. If you're afraid that gang may trail you here and start raising the devil—how many are there?"

"Five."

"I'm as good with a gun as I ever was in the old days. So is Buck. Partner, let's make the show down together. Stick here with Kate and Joan and Buck and I will help you hold the fort. Don't look at me like that. I mean it. Do you think I've forgotten what you did for me that night in Elkhead? Not in a thousand years. Dan, I'd rather make my last play here than any other place in the world. Let 'em come! We'll salt them down and plant them where they won't grow."

As he talked the pallor quite left him, and the fighting fire blazed in his eyes, he stood lion-like, his feet spread apart as if to meet a shock, his tawny head thrown back, and there was about him a hair-trigger sensitiveness, in spite of his bulk, a nervousness of hand and coldness of glance which characterizes the gun-fighter. Buck Daniels stepped closer, without a word, but one felt that he also had walked into the alliance. As Barry watched them the yellow which swirled in his eyes flickered away for a moment.

"Why, gents," he murmured, "they ain't any call for trouble. The posse? What's that got to do with me? Our accounts are all squared up."

The two stared dumbly.

"They killed Grey Molly; I killed one of them."

"A horse—for a man?" repeated Lee Haines, breathing hard.

"A life for a life," said Dan simply. "They got no call for complainin'."

Glances of wonder, glances of meaning, flashed back and forth from Haines to Buck.

"Well, then," said the latter, and he took in Kate with

a caution from the corner of his eye, "if that's the case, let's sit down and chin for a minute."

Dan stood with his head bowed a little, frowning; two forces pulled him, and Kate leaned against the wall off in the shadow with her eyes closed, waiting, waiting, waiting through the crisis.

"I'd like to stay and chin with you, Buck—but, I got to be off. Out there—in the night—something may happen before mornin'." Black Bart licked the hand of the master and whined. "Easy, boy. We're startin'."

"But the night's just beginnin'," said Buck Daniels genially. "You got a world of time before you, and with Satan to fall back on you don't have to count your minutes. Pull up a chair beside me, Dan, and——"

The latter shook his head, decided. "Buck, I can't do it. Just to sit here"——he looked about him—"makes me feel sort of choked. Them walls are as close—as a coffin."

He was already turning; Kate straightened in the shadow, desperate.

"As a matter of fact, Dan," said Lee Haines, suddenly, "we need your help badly."

"Help?"

The heart of Kate stood in her eyes as she looked at Lee Haines.

"Sit down a minute, Dan, and I'll tell you about it."

Barry slipped into a chair which he had pulled to one side—so that the back of it was towards the wall, and every one in the room was before him.

CHAPTER XIV

Suspense

The help which Lee Haines wanted, it turned out, was guidance across a difficult stretch of country which he and Buck Daniels wanted to prospect, and while he talked Barry listened uneasily. It was constitutionally impossible for him to say no when a favor was asked of him, and Haines counted heavily on that characteristic; in the meantime Black Bart lay on the hearth with his wistful eyes turned steadily up to the master; and Buck Daniels went to Kate on the farther side of the room. She sat quivering, alternately crushing and soothing Joan with the strength of her caresses. Buck drew a chair close, with his back half towards the fire.

"Turn around a little, Kate," he cautioned. "Don't let Dan see your face."

She obeyed him automatically.

"Is there a hope, Buck? What have I done to deserve this? I don't want to live; I want to die! I want to die!"

"Steady, steady!" he cut in, and his face was working. "If you keep on like this you'll bust down in a minute or two. And you know what tears do to Dan; he'll be out of this house like a scairt coyote. Brace up!"

She struggled and won a partial control.

"I'm fighting hard, Buck."

"Fight harder still. You ought to know him better than I do. When he's like this it drives him wild to have other folks thinkin' about him."

He looked over to Dan. In spite of the bowed head of the latter as he listened to Haines yarning he gave an impression of electric awareness to all that was around him.

"Talk soft," whispered Buck. "Maybe he knows we're talkin' about him."

He raised his voice out of the whisper, breaking in on a sentence about Joan, as if this were the tenor of their talk. Then he lowered his tone again.

"Think quick. Talk soft. Do you want Dan kept here?"

"For God's sake, yes."

"Suppose the posse gets him here?"

"We musn't dodge the law."

They were gauging their voices with the closest precision. Talking like this so close to Barry was like dancing among flasks of nitroglycerine. Once, and once only, Lee Haines cast a desperate eye across to them, begging them to come to his rescue, then he went back to his talk with Dan, raising his voice to shelter the conference of the other two.

"If they come, he'll fight."

"No, he isn't at the fighting pitch yet, I know!"

"If you're wrong they'll be dead men here."

"He sees no difference between the death of a horse and the death of a man. He feels that the law has no score against him. He'll go quietly."

"And we'll find ways of fightin' the law?"

"Yes, but it needs money."

"I've got a stake."

"God bless you, Buck."

"Take my advice."

"What?"

"Let him go now."

She glanced at him wildly.

"Kate, he's gone already."

"No, no, no!"

"I say he's gone. Look at his eyes."

"I don't dare."

"The yaller is comin' up in 'em. He's wild again."

She shook her head in mute agony. Buck Daniels groaned, softly.

"Then they's goin' to be a small-sized hell started around this cabin before mornin'."

He got up and went slowly back towards the fire. Lee Haines was talking steadily, leisurely, going round and round his subject again and again, and Barry listened with bowed head, but his eyes were fixed upon those of the wolf-dog at his feet. When he grew restless, Haines chained him to the chair with some direct question, yet it was a hard game to play. All this time the posse might be gathering around the cabin; and the forehead of Haines whitened and glistened with sweat. His voice was the only living thing in the cabin, after a time, sketching his imaginary plans for the benefit of Barry—his voice and the wistful eyes of Joan which kept steadily on Daddy Dan. Something had come between them and lifted a barrier which she could not understand, and with all her aching child's heart she wondered at it.

For the second time that evening the wolf stood up on the hearth, but he was not yet on his feet before Dan was out of his chair and standing close to the wall, where the shadows swallowed him. Lee Haines sat with his lips frozen on the next unspoken word. Two shadows, whose feet made no sound, Black Bart and Dan glided to the door and peered into the night; then Barry went back, step by step, until his back was once more to the wall. Not until that instant did the others hear. It was a step which approached behind the house; a loud rap at the back door.

It was the very loudness of the knock which made Kate draw a breath of relief; if it had been a stealthy tap she would have screamed. He who rapped did not wait for an answer; they heard the door creak open, the sound of a heavy man's step.

"It's Vic," said Dan quietly, and then the door opened which led into the kitchen and the tall form of Gregg entered. He paused there.

"Here I am again, ma'am."

"Good evening," she answered faintly.

He cleared his throat, embarrassed.

'Darned if I didn't play a fool game to-day—hello, Dan."

The other nodded.

"Rode in a plumb circle and come back where I started." He laughed, and the laughter broke off a little shortly. He stepped to the wall and hung up his bridle on its peg, which is the immemorial manner of asking hospitality in the mountain-desert. "Hope I ain't puttin' you out, Kate. I see you got company."

She started, recalled from her thoughts.

"Excuse me, Vic. Vic Gregg, Buck Daniels, Lee Haines."

They shook hands, and Vic detained Haines a moment.

"Seems to me I've heard of you, Haines."

"Maybe."

Gregg looked at the big man narrowly, and then swung back towards Dan. He knew many things, now. Lee Haines—yes, that was the name. One of the crew who followed Jim Silent; and Dan Barry? What a fool he had been not to remember! It was Dan Barry who had gone on the trail of Silent's gang and hounded it to death; Lee Haines alone had been spared. Yes, half a dozen years before the mountain-folk had heard that story, a wild and improbable one. It fitted in with what Pete Glass had told him of the shooting of Harry Fisher; it explained a great deal which had mystified him since he first met Barry; it made the thing he had come to do at once easier and harder.

"I s'pose Molly showed a clean pair of heels to the whole lot of 'em?" he said to Dan.

"She's dead."

"Dead?" His astonishment was well enough affected. "God A'mighty, Dan, not Grey Molly—my hoss?"

"Dead. I shot her."

Vic gasped. "You?"

"They'd busted her leg. I put her out of pain."

Gregg dropped into a chair. It was not altogether an affectation, not altogether a piece of skilful acting now, for though the sheriff had told him all that happened he had not had a chance to feel the truth; but now it swept over him, all her tricks, all her deviltry, all that long companionship. His head bowed.

No smile touched the faces of the others in the room, but a reverent silence fell on the room. Then that figure among the shadows moved out, stepped to the side of Vic, and a light hand rested on his shoulder. The other looked up, haggard.

82

"She's gone, partner," Dan said gently, "but she's paid for."

"Paid for? Dan, they ain't any money could pay me back for Grey Molly."

"I know; I know! Not that way, but there was a life given for a life."

"Eh?"

"One man died for Molly."

As the meaning came home to Gregg he blinked, and then, looking up, he found a change in the eyes of Barry, for they seemed to be lighted from within, coldly, and his glance went down to the very bottom of Vic's soul, probing. It was only an instant, a thing of which Gregg could not make sure, and then Dan slipped back into his place among the shadows by the wall. But a chill sense of guilt, a premonition of danger, stayed in Gregg. The palms of his hands grew moist.

CHAPTER XV

Seven for One

Dangerous men were no novelty for Gregg. He had lived with them, worked with them, as hard-fisted himself an any, and as ready for trouble, but the man of the mountain-desert has a peculiar dread for the practiced, known gun-fighter. In the days of the rapier when the art of fence grew so complicated that half a life was needed for its mastery, men would as soon commit suicide as ruffle it with an assured duellist; and the man of the mountain-desert has a similar respect for those who are born, it might be said, gun in hand. There was ample reason for the prickling in his scalp. Vic felt, for here he sat on an errand of consummate danger with three of these deadly fighters. Two of them he knew by name and repute, however dimly, and as for Buck Daniels, unless all signs failed the dark, sharp-eyed fellow was hardly less grim than the others. Vic gauged the three one by one. Daniels might be dreaded for an outburst of wild temper and in that moment he could be as terrible as any. Lee Haines would fight coolly, his blue eyes never clouded by passion, for that was his repute as the right hand man of Jim Silent, in the days when Jim had been a terrible, half-legendary figure. One felt that same quiet strength as the tawny haired man talked to Barry now; his voice was a smooth, deep current. But as for Barry himself, Gregg could not compute the factors which entered into the man. By all outward seeming that slender, half-timid figure was not a tithe of the force which either of the others repre-sented, but out of the past Gregg's memory gathered more and more details, clear and clearer, of the wolf-dog, the black stallion, and the whistling man who tracked down

Silent—"Whistling Dan" Barry; that was what they called him, sometimes! Nothing was definite in the mind of Gregg. The stories consisted of patched details, heard here and there at third or fourth hand, but he remembered one epic incident in which Barry had ridden, so rumor told, into the very heart of Elkhead, taken from the jail this very man, this Lee Haines, and carried him through the cordon of every armed man in Elkhead. And there was another picture, dimmer still, which an eye witness had painted: of how, at an appointed hour, Barry met Jim Silent and killed him.

Out of these thoughts he glanced again at the man in the shadow, half expecting to find his host swollen to giant size. Instead, he found the same meager form, the same old suggestion of youth which would not age, the same pale hands, of almost feminine litheness. Lee Haines talked on—about a porphyry dyke somewhere to the north—a ledge to be found in the space of ten thousand square miles—a list of vague clues—an appeal for Barry to help them find it—and Barry was held listening though ever seeming to drift, or about to drift, towards the door. Black Bart lay facing his master, and his snaky head followed every movement. Kate sat where the firelight barely touched on her, and in her arms she held Joan, whose face and great bright eyes were turned towards Daddy Dan. All things in the room centered on the place where the man sat by the wall, and the sense of something impending swept over Gregg; then a wild fear—did they know the danger outside? He must make conversation; he turned to Kate, but at the same moment the voice of Buck Daniels beside him, close.

"I know how you feel, old man. I remember an old bay hoss of mine, a Morgan hoss, and when he died I grieved for near onto a year, mostly. He wasn't much of a hoss to look at, too long coupled, you'd say, and his legs was short, but he got about like a coyote and when he sat down on a rope you couldn't budge him with a team of Percherons. That's how good he was! When he was a four year old I was cutting out yearlin's with him, and how——"

The loud, cheerful tone fell away to a confidential

murmur, Daniels leaned closer, with a smile of prospective humor, but the words which came to Gregg were "Partner, if I was you I'd get up and git and I wouldn't stop till I put a hell of a long ways between me and this cabin!"

It spoke well of Vic's nerve that no start betrayed him. He bowed his head a little, as though to catch the trend of the jolly story better, nodding.

"What's wrong?" he muttered back.

"Barry's watchin' you out of the shadow."

Then: "You fool, don't look!"

But there was method in Vic's raising his head. He threw it back and broke into laughter, but while he laughed he searched the shadow by the wall where Dan sat, and he felt glimmering eyes fixed steadily upon him. He dropped his head again, as if to hear more.

"What's it mean, Daniels?"

"You ought to know. I don't. But he don't mean you no good. He's lookin' at you too steady. If I was you——"

Through the whisper of Buck, through the loud, steady talk of Lee Haines, cut the voice of Barry.

"Vic!"

The latter looked up and found that Barry was standing just within the glow of the hearth-light and something about him made Gregg's heart shrink.

"Vic, how much did they pay you?"

He tried to answer; he would have given ten years of his life to have his voice under control for an instant; but his tongue froze. He knew that every one had turned toward him and he tried to smile, look unconcerned, but in spite of himself his eyes were wide, fixed, and he felt that they could stare into the bottom of his soul and see the guilt.

"How much?"

Then his voice came, but he could have groaned when he heard its crazily shaken, shrill sound.

"What d'you mean, Dan?"

The other smiled and Gregg added hastily: "If you want me to be movin' along, Dan, of course you're the doctor."

"How much did they pay?" repeated the quiet, inexorable voice.

He could have stood that, even without much fear, for no matter how terrible the man might be in action his hands were tied in his own house; but now Kate spoke: "Vic, what have you done?"

Then it came, in a flood. Hot shame rolled through him and the words burst out:

"I'm a yaller houn-dog, a sneakin' no-good cur! Dan, you're right. I've sold you. They're out there, all of 'em, waitin' in the rocks. For God's sake take my gun and pump me full of lead!"

He threw his arms out, clear of his holster and turned that Barry might draw his revolver. Vaguely he knew that Haines and Buck had drawn swiftly close to him from either side; vaguely he heard the cry of Kate; but all that he clearly understood was the merciless, unmoved face of Barry. It was pretense; with all his being he wanted to die, but when Barry made no move to strike he turned desperately to the others.

"Do the job for him. He saved my life and then I used it to sell him. Daniels, Haines, I got no use for livin'."

"Vic," he said, "take—this!—and march to your friends outside; and when you get through them, plant a forty-five slug in your own dirty heart and then rot." Haines held out his gun with a gesture of contempt.

But Kate slipped in front of him, white and anguished.

"It was the girl you told me about, Vic?" she said. "You did it to get back to her?"

He dropped his head.

"Dan, let him go!"

"I got no thought of usin' him."

"Why not?" cried Vic suddenly. "I'll do the way Haines said. Or else let me stay here and fight 'em off with you. Dan, for God's sake give me one chance to make good."

It was like talking to a face of stone.

"The door's open for you, and waitin'. One thing before you go. That's the same gang you told me about before? Ronicky Joe, Harry Fisher, Gus Reeve, Mat Henshaw, Sliver Waldron and Pete Glass?"

"Harry Fisher's dead, Dan, if you'll give me one fightin' chance to play square now——"

"Tell 'em that I know 'em. Tell 'em one thing more. I thought Grey Molly was worth only one man. But I was wrong. They've done me dirt and played crooked. They come huntin' me—with a decoy. Now tell 'em from me that Grey Molly is worth seven men, and she's goin' to be paid for in full."

He stepped to the wall and took down the bridle which Vic had hung there.

"I guess you'll be needin' this?"

It ended all talk; it even seemed to Gregg that as soon as he received the bridle from the hand of Barry the truce ended with a sudden period and war began. He turned slowly away.

CHAPTER XVI

Man-Hunting

As Vic Gregg left the house, the new moon peered at him over a black mountain-top, a sickle of white with a half imaginary line rounding the rest of the circle, and to the shaken mind of Vic it seemed as if a ghostly spectator had come out to watch the tragedy among the peaks. At the line of the rocks the sheriff spoke.

"Gregg, you've busted your contract. You didn't bring him out."

Vic threw his revolver on the ground.

"I bust the rest of it here and now. I'm through. Put on your irons and take me back. Hang me and be damned to you, but I'll do no more to double-cross him."

Sliver Waldron drew from his pocket something which jangled faintly, but the sheriff stopped him with a word. He sat up behind his rock.

"I got an idea, Gregg, that you've finished up your job and double-crossed *us!* Does he know that I'm out here? Sit down there out of sight."

"I'll do that," said Gregg, obeying, "because you got the right to make me, but you ain't got the right to make me talk, and nothin' this side of hell can pry a word out of me!"

The sheriff drew down his brows until his eyes were merely cavities of blackness. Very tenderly he fondled the rifle-butt which lay across his knees, and never in the mountain-desert had there been a more humbly unpretentious figure of a man.

He said: "Vic, I been thinkin' that you had the man-sized makin's of a skunk, but I'm considerable glad to see

I've judged you wrong. Sit quiet here. I ain't goin' to put no irons on you if you give me your parole."

"I'll see you in hell before I give you nothin'! I was a man, or a partways man, till I met up with you to-night, and now I'm a houn'-dog that's done my partner dirt! God A'mighty, what made me do it?"

He beat his knuckles against his forehead.

"What you've done you can't undo," answered the sheriff. "Vic, I've seen gents do considerable worse than you've done and come clean afterwards. You're goin' to get off for what you've done to Blondy, and you're goin' to live straight afterwards. You're goin' to get married and you're goin' to play white. Why, man, I had to use you as far as I could. But d'you think I *wanted* you to bring me out Barry? You couldn't look Betty square in the face if you'd done what you set out to do. Now, I ain't pressin' you, but I done some scouting while you was away, and I heard four men's voices in the house. Can you tell me who's there?"

"You've played square, Pete," answered Vic hoarsely, "and I'll do my part. Go down and get on your hosses and ride like hell; because in ten minutes you're goin' to have three bad ones around your necks."

A mutter came from the rest of the posse, for this was rather more than they had planned ahead. The sheriff, however, only sighed, and as the moonlight increased Vic could see that he was deeply, childishly contented, for in the heart of the little dusty man there was that inextinguishable spark, the love of battle. Chance had thrown him on the side of the law, but sooner or later dull times were sure to come and then Pete Glass would cut out work of his own making—go bad. The love of the man-trail is a passion that works in two ways, and they who begin by hunting will in the end be the hunted; the mountain-desert is filled with such histories.

"Three to five," said the sheriff, "sounds more interestin', Vic."

A sudden passion to destroy that assured calm rose in Gregg.

"Three common men might make you a game," he said, glowering, "but them ain't common ones. One of 'em I don't know, but he has a damned nervous hand. Another is Lee Haines!"

He had succeeded in part, at least. The sheriff sat bolt erect; he seemed to be hearing distant music.

"Lee Haines!" he murmured. "That was Jim Silent's man. They say he was as fast with a gun as Jim himself." He sighed again. "They's nothing like a big man, Vic, to fill your sights."

"Daniels and Haines, suppose you count them off agin the rest of your gang, Pete. That leaves Barry for you." He grinned maliciously. "D'you know what Barry it is?"

"It's a kind of common name, Vic."

"Pete, have you heard of Whistlin' Dan?"

No doubt about it, he had burst the confidence of the sheriff into fragments. The little man began to pant and even in the dim light Vic could see that his face was working.

"Him!" he said at length, And then: "I might of knowed! Him!" He leaned closer. "Keep it to yourself, Vic, or you'll have the rest of the boys runnin' for cover before the fun begins."

He snuggled a little closer to his rock and turned his head towards the house.

"Him!" he said again.

Columbus, when he saw the land of his dream wavering blue in the distance, might have hailed it with such a heart-filling whisper, and Vic knew that when these two met, these two slender, small men with the uneasy hands, there would be a battle whose fame would ring from range to range.

"If they was only a bit more light," muttered the sheriff. "My God, Vic, why ain't the moon just a mite nearer the full!"

After that, not a word for a long time until the lights in the house were suddenly extinguished.

"So they won't show up agin no background when they make their run," murmured the sheriff. He pushed up his hat brim so that it covered his eyes more perfectly. "Boys, get ready. They're comin' now!"

Mat Henshaw took up the word, and repeated it, and

91

the whisper ran down the line of men who lay irregularly among the rocks, until at last Sliver Waldron brought it to a stop with a deep murmur. Not even a whisper could altogether disguise his booming bass. It seemed to Vic Gregg that the air about him grew more tense; his arm muscles commenced to ache from the gripping of his hands. Then a door creaked—they could tell the indubitable sound as if there were a light to see it swing cautiously wide.

"They're goin' out the back way," interpreted the sheriff, "but they'll come around in front. They ain't any other way they can get out of here. Pass that down the line, Mat."

Before the whisper had trailed out half its course, a woman screamed in the house. It sent a jag of lightning through the brain of Vic Gregg; he started up.

"Get down," commanded the sheriff curtly. "Or they'll plant you."

"For God's sake, Pete, he's killin' his wife—Kate—he's gone mad—I seen it comin' in his eyes!"

"Shut up," muttered Glass, "an' listen."

A pulse of sound floated out to them, and stopped the breath of Gregg; it was a deep, stifled sobbing.

"She's begged him to stay with her; he's gone," said the sheriff. "Now it'll come quick."

But the sheriff was wrong. There was not a sound, not a sign of a rush.

Presently: "What sort of a lass is she, Gregg?"

"All yaller hair, Pete, and the softes' blue eyes you ever see."

The sheriff made no answer, but Vic saw the little bony hand tense about the barrel of the rifle. Still that utter quiet, with the pulse of the sobbing lying like a weight upon the air, and the horror of the waiting mounted and grew, like peak upon peak before the eyes of the climber.

"Watch for 'em sneakin' up on us through the rocks. Watch for 'em close, lads. It ain't goin' to be a rush."

Once more the sibilant murmur ran down the line, and the voice of Sliver Waldron brought it faintly to a period.

"Three of 'em," continued the sheriff, "and most likely they'll come at us three ways."

Through the shadow Vic watched the lips of Glass work and caught the end of his soft murmur to himself: ". . . . all three!"

He understood; the sheriff had offered up a deep prayer that all three might fall by his gun.

"Up from the farther end of the line the whisper ran lightly, swiftly, with a stammer of haste in it: "To the right!"

Ay, there to the right, gliding from the corner of the house, went a dark form, and then another, and disappeared among the rocks. They had offered not enough target for even chance shooting.

"Hold for close range" ordered the sheriff, and the order was repeated. However much he might wish to win all the glory of the fray, the sheriff took no chances—threw none of his odds away. He was a methodical man.

A slight patter caught the ear of Vic, like the running of many small children over a heavy carpet, and then two shades blew around the side of the house, one small and scudding close to the ground, the other vastly larger—a man on horseback. It seemed a naked horse, at first, so close to the back did the rider lean, and before Vic could see clearly the vision burst on them all. Several things kept shots from being fired earlier.

The first alarm had called attention to the opposite side of the house from that on which the rider appeared; then, the moon gave only a vague, treacherous light, and the black horse blended into it—the grass lightened the fall of his racing feet.

Like a ship driving through a fog they rushed into view, the black stallion, and Bart fleeting in front, and the surprise was complete. Vic could see it work even in the sheriff, for the latter, having his rifle trained towards his right jerked it about with a short curse and blazed at the new target, again, again, and the line of the posse joined the fire. Before the crack of their guns went from the ears of Vic, long before the echoes bellowed back from the hills, Satan leaped high up. Perhaps that change of position saved both it and its rider. Straight across the pale moon drove the body with head stretched forth, ears back, feet gathered close—a winged horse with a buoyant figure upon it. It cleared a five foot rock, and rushed instantly out of view among the boulders. The fugitive had fired only one shot, and that when the stallion was at the crest of its leap.

CHAPTER XVII

The Second Man

The sheriff was on his feet, whining with eagerness and with the rest of his men he sent a shower of lead splashing vainly into the deeper night beside the mountain, where the path wound down.

"It's done! Hold up, lads!" called Pete Glass. "He's beat us!"

The firing ceased, and they heard the rush of the hoofs along the graveled slope and the clanging on rocks.

"It's done," repeated the sheriff. "How?"

And he stood staring blankly, with a touch of horror in his face.

"By God, Mat's plugged."

"Mat Henshaw? Who———"

"Clean through the head."

He lay in an oddly twisted heap, as though every bone in his body were broken, and when they drew him about they found the red mark in his forehead and even made out the dull surprise in his set face. There had been no pain in that death, the second for the sake of Grey Molly.

"The other two!" said the sheriff, more to himself than to Vic, who stood beside him.

"Easy, Pete," he cautioned. "You got nothin' agin Haines and Daniels."

The sheriff flashed at him that hungry, baffled glance.

"Maybe I can find something. You Gregg, keep your mouth shut and stand back. Halloo!"

He sent a long call quavering between the lonely mountains.

"You yonder—Lee Haines! D'you give up to the law?"

A burst of savage laughter flung back at him, and then: "Why the hell should I?"

"Haines, I give you fair warnin'! For resistin' the law and interferin', I ask you, do you surrender?"

"Who are you?"

The big voice fairly swallowed the rather shrill tone of the sheriff.

"I'm sheriff Pete Glass."

"You lie. Whoever heard of a sheriff come sneakin' round like a coyote lookin' for dead meat?"

Pete Glass grinned with rage.

"Haines, you ain't much better'n spoiled meat if you keep back. I give you till I count ten——"

"Why, you bob-tailed skunk," shouted a new voice. "You bone-spavined, pink-eyed rat-catcher," continued this very particular describer, "what have you got on us? Come out and dicker and we'll do the same!"

The sheriff sighed, softly, deeply.

"I thought maybe they wouldn't get down to talk," he murmured. But since the last chance for a battle was gone, he stepped fearlessly from behind his rock and advanced into the open. Two tall figures came to meet him.

"Now," said Lee Haines, stalking forward. "One bad move, just the glint of a single gun from the rest of you sheep thieves, and I'll tame your pet sheriff and send him to hell for a model."

They halted, close to each other, the two big men, Haines in the front, and the sheriff.

"You're Lee Haines?"

"You've named me."

"And you're Buck Daniels?"

"That's me."

"Gents, you've resisted an officer of the law in the act of makin' an arrest. I s'pose you know what that means?"

Big Lee Haines laughed.

"Don't start a bluff, sheriff. I know a bit about the law."

"Maybe by experience?"

It was an odd thing to watch the three, every one of them a practiced fighter, every one of them primed for trouble, but each ostentatiously keeping his hands away from the holsters.

"What we might have done if we had come to a pinch," said Haines, "is one thing, and what we did do is another. Barry was started and off before we had a chance to show teeth, my friend, and you never even caught the flash of our guns. If he'd waited—but he didn't. There's nothing left for us to do except say good-by."

The little dusty man stroked his moustaches thoughtfully. He had gone out there hoping against hope that his chance might come—to trick the two into violence, even to start an arrest for reasons which he knew his posse would swear to; but it must be borne in mind that Pete Glass was a careful man by instinct. Taking in probable speed of hand and a thousand other details at a glance, Pete sensed the danger of these two and felt in his heart of hearts that he was more than master of either of them, considered alone; better than Buck Daniels by an almost safe margin of steadiness—better than Lee Haines by a flickering instant of speed. Had either of them alone faced him, he would have taken his chance, perhaps, to kill or be killed, for the long trail and the escape had fanned that spark within him to a cold, hungry fire; but to attempt a play with both at the same time was death, and he knew it. Seeing that the game was up, he laid his cards on the table with characteristic frankness.

"Gents," he said, "I reckon you've come clean with me. You ain't my meat and I ain't goin' to clutter up your way. Besides"—even in the dull moonshine they caught the humorous glint of his eyes—"a friend is a friend, and I'll say I'm glad that you didn't step into the shady side of the law while Barry was gettin' away."

No one could know what it cost Pete Glass to be genial at that instant, for this night he felt that he had just missed the great moment which he had yearned for since the day when he learned to love the kick of a six-shooter against the heel of his hand. It was the desire to meet face to face one whose metal of will and mind was equal to his own, whose nerves were electric energies perfectly under command, whose muscles were fine spun steel. He had gone half a life-time on the trail of fighters and always he had known that when the crisis came his hand would be the swifter, his eye the more steady; the trailing was a delight always, but the actual kill was a matter of slaughter rather than a game of hazard. Only the rider of the black stallion had given him the sense of equal power, and his whole soul had risen for the great chance of all. That chance was gone; he pushed the thought of it away—for the time—and turned back to the business at hand.

"They's only one thing," he went on. "Sliver! Ronicky! Step along, gents, and we'll have a look at the insides of that house."

"Steady!" broke in Haines. He barred the path to the front door. "Sheriff, you don't know me, but I'm going to ask you to take my word for what's in that house."

Glass swept him with a look of a new nature.

"I got an idea your word might do. Well, what's in the house?"

"A little five-year-old girl and her mother; nothing else worth seeing."

"Nothing else," considered the sheriff, "but that's quite a lot. Maybe his wife could tell me where he's going? Give me an idea where I might call on him?"

"Partner, you can't see her."

"Can't?"

"No, by God!"

"H-m-m!" murmured the sheriff. He watched the big man plant himself, swaying a little on his feet as though poising for action, and beside him a slightly smaller figure not less determined.

"That girl in there is old man Cumberland's daughter," said Daniels, "and no matter what her—what Dan Barry may be, Kate Cumberland is white folks."

The sheriff remembered what Vic had said of yellow hair and soft blue eyes.

"Leastways," he said, "she seems to have a sort of way with the men."

"Sheriff you're on a cold trail," said Haines. "Inside the house is just a heart-broken girl and her baby. If you want to see them—go ahead!"

"She might know something," mused the sheriff, "and I s'pose I'd ought to pry it out of her right now: but I don't care for that sort of pickin's." He repeated softly: "A girl and a baby!" and turned on his heel. "All right, boys, climb your hosses. Two of you take Matt. We'll bury him where we put Harry. I guess we can pack him that far."

"How's that?" This from Haines. "One of your gang dropped?"

"He is."

They followed him and stood presently beside the body. Aside from the red mark in the forehead he seemed asleep, and smiling at some pleasant dream; a handsome fellow in the strength of first manhood, this man who was the second to die for Grey Molly.

"It's the end of Dan Barry," said Buck. "Lee, we'll never have Whistlin' Dan for a friend again. He's wild for good."

The sheriff turned and eyed him closely.

He's got to come back," said Haines. "He's got to come back for the sake of Kate."

"He'd better be dead for the sake of Kate," answered Buck.

"Why, partner, this isn't the first time he's gone wild."

"Don't you see, Lee?"

"Well?"

"He's fighting to kill. He's shooting to kill, and he ain't ever done that before. He crippled his men; he put 'em out of the way with a busted leg or a plugged shoulder; but now he's out to finish 'em. Lee, he'll never come back."

He looked to the white face of Vic Gregg, standing by, and he said without anger; "Maybe it ain't your fault, but you've started a pile of harm. Look at these gents around you, the sheriff and all—they're no better'n dead, Gregg, and that's all along of you. Barry has started on the trail of all of you. Look at that house back there. It's packed full of hell, and all along of you. Lee, let's get back. I'm feelin' sick inside."

CHAPTER XVIII

Concerning the Strength of Women

There were three things discussed by Lee Haines and Buck Daniels in the dreary days which followed. The first was to keep on their way across the mountains and cut themselves away from the sorrow of that cabin. The second was to strike the trail of Barry and hunt until they found his refuge and attempt to lead him back to his family. The third was simply to stay on and where they found the opportunity, help Kate. They discarded the first idea without much talk; it would be yellow, they decided, and the debt they owed to the Dan Barry of the old days was too great to be shouldered off so easily: they cast away the second thought still more quickly, for the trail which baffled the shrewd sheriff, as they knew, would be too much for them. It remained to stay with Kate, making excursions through the mountains from day to day to maintain the pretence of carrying on their own business, and always at hand in time of need.

It was no easy part to play, for in the house they found Kate more and more silent, more and more thoughtful, never speaking of her trouble, but behind her eyes a ghost of waiting that haunted them. If the wind shrilled down the pass, if a horse neighed from the corral, there was always the start in her, the thrill of hope, and afterwards the pitiful deadening of her smile. She was not less beautiful they thought, as she grew paler, but the terrible silence of the place drove them away time and again. Even Joan no longer pattered about the house, and when they came down out of the mountains they never heard her shrill laughter. She sat cross-legged by the hearth in her old place during the evenings with her chin resting on one hand and her eyes fixed wistfully upon the fire; and some times they found her on the little hillock behind the house, from the top of which she could view every approach to the cabin. Of Dan and even of Black Bart, her playmate she soon learned not to speak, for the mention of them made her mother shrink and whiten. Indeed, the saddest thing in that house was the quiet in which the child waited, waited, waited, and never spoke.

"She ain't more'n a baby," said Buck Daniels, "and you can leave it to time to make her forget."

"But," growled Lee Haines, "Kate isn't a baby. Buck, it drives me damn near crazy to see her fade this way."

"Now you lay to this," answered Buck. "She'll pull through. She'll never forget, maybe, but she'll go on livin' for the sake of the kid."

"You know a hell of a lot about women, don't you?" said Haines.

"I know enough, son," nodded Buck.

He had, in fact, reduced women to a few distinct categories, and he only waited to place a girl in her particular class before he felt quite intimate acquaintance with her entire mind and soul.

"It'll kill her," pronounced Lee Haines. "Why, she's like a flower, Buck, and sorrow will cut her off at the root. Think of a girl like that thrown away in these damned deserts! It makes me sick—sick! She ought to have nothing but velvet to touch—nothing but a millionaire for a husband, and never a worry in her life." He grew excited. "But here's the flower thrown away and the heel crushing it without mercy."

"Buck Daniels regarded him with pity.

"I feel kind of sorry for you, Lee, when I hear you talk about girls. No wonder they make a fool of you. A flower crushed under the foot, eh? You just listen to me, my boy. You and me figure to be pretty hard, don't we? Well, soft pine stacked up agin quartzite, is what we are compared to Kate."

Lee Haines gaped at him, too astonished to be angry. He suggested softening of the brain to Buck, but the latter waved aside the implications.

"Now, supposin' Kate was one of these dark girls with

102

eyes like black diamonds and a lot of snap and zip to her. If she was like that I s'pose you'd figure her to forget all about Dan inside of a month—and maybe marry you?"

"You be damned!"

"Maybe I am. Them hard, snappy lookin' girls are the ones that smash. They're brittle, that's why; but you take a soft lookin' girl like Kate, maybe she ain't a diamond point to cut glass, but she's tempered steel that'll bend, and bend, and bend, and then when you wait for it to break it flips up and knocks you down. That's Kate."

Lee Haines rolled a cigarette in silence. He was too disgusted to answer, until his first puff of smoke dissolved Buck in a cloud of thin blue.

"You ought to sing to a congregation instead of to cows, Buck. You have the tune, and you might get by in a church; but cows have sense."

"Kate will buckle and bend and fade for a while," went on Buck, wholly unperturbed, "but just when you go out to pick daisies for her you'll come back and find her singing to the stove. Her strength is down deep, like some of these outlaw hosses that got a filmy, sleepy lookin' eye. They save their hell till you sink the spurs in 'em. You think she loves Dan, don't you?"

"I have a faint suspicion of it," sneered Haines. "I suppose I'm wrong?"

"You are."

"Buck, I may have slipped a nickel into you, but you're playing the wrong tune. Knock off and talk sense, will you?"

"When you grow up, son, you'll understand some of the things I'm tryin' to explain in words of one syllable. She don't love Dan. She thinks she does, but down deep they ain't a damned thing in the world she gives a rap about exceptin' Joan. Men? What are they to her? Marriage? That's simply an accident that's needed so she can have a baby. Delicate, shrinkin' flower, is she? I tell you, my boy if it was necessary for Joan she'd tear out your heart and mine and send Dan plumb to hell. You fasten on to them words, because they're gospel."

It was late afternoon while they talked, and they were swinging slowly down a gulch towards the home cabin.

At that very time Kate, from the door of the house where she sat, saw a dark form slink from rock to rock at the rim of the little plateau, a motion so swift that it flicked through the corner of her eye, a thing to be sensed rather than seen. She set up very stiff, her lips white as chalk, but nothing more stirred. A few minutes later, when her heart was beating almost at normal she heard Joan scream from behind the house, not in terror, or pain, as her keen mother-ear knew perfectly well, but with a wild delight. She whipped about the corner of the house and there she saw Joan with her pudgy arms around the neck of Black Bart.

"Bart! Dear old Bart! Has he come? Has he come?"

And she strained her eyes against the familiar mountains around her as if she would force her vision through rock. There was no trace of Dan, no sign or sound when she would even have welcomed the eerie whistle. The wolf-dog was already at play with Joan. She was on his back and he darted off in an effortless gallop, winding to and fro among the rocks. Most children would have toppled among the stones at the first of his swerves, but Joan clung like a burr, both hands dug into his hair, shrieking with excitement. Sometimes she reeled and almost slid at one of those lightning turns, for the game was to almost unseat her, but just as she was sliding off Bart would slacken his pace and let her find a firm seat once more. They wound farther and farther away, and suddenly Kate cried, terror-stricken: "Joan! Come back!"

A tug at the ear of the wolf-dog swung them around; then as they approached, the fear left the mind of the mother and a new thought came in its place. She coaxed Joan from Bart—they could play later on, she promised, to their heart's desire—and led her into the house. Black Bart followed to the door, but not all their entreaty or scolding could make him cross the threshold. He merely snarled at Kate, and even Joan's tugging at his ears could not budge him. He stood canting his head and watching them wistfully while Kate changed Joan's clothes.

She dessed her as if for a festival, with a blue bonnet that let the yellow hair curl out from the edges, and a little blue cloak, and shiny boots incredibly small, and around the bonnet she laid a wreath of yellow wild flowers. Then she wrote her letter, closed it in an envelope, and fastened it securely in the pocket of the cloak.

She drew Joan in front of her and held her by both hands.

"Joan, darling," she said, "munner wants you to go with Bart up through the mountains. Will you be afraid?"

A very decided shake of the head answered her, for Joan's eyes were already over her shoulder looking towards the big dog. And she was a little sullen at these unnecessary words.

"It might grow dark," she said. "You wouldn't care?"

Here Joan became a little dubious, but a whine from Bart seemed to reassure her.

"Bart will keep Joan," she said.

"He will. And he'll take you up through the rocks to Daddy Dan."

The face of the child grew brilliant.

"Daddy Dan?" she whispered.

"And when you get to him, take this little paper out of your pocket and give it to him. You won't forget?"

"Give the paper to Daddy Dan," repeated Joan solemnly.

Kate dropped to her knees and gathered the little body close, close, until Joan cried out, but when she was released the child reached up an astonished hand, touched the face of Kate with awe, and then stared at her finger tips.

A moment later, Joan stood in front of Black Bart, with the head of the wolf-dog seized firmly between her hands while she frowned intently into his face.

"Take Joan to Daddy Dan," she ordered.

At the name, the sharp ears pricked; a speaking intelligence grew up in his eyes.

"Giddap," commanded Joan, when she was in position on the back of Bart. And she thumped her heels against the furry ribs.

Towards Kate, who stood trembling in the door, Bart cast the departing favor of a throat-tearing growl, and then shambled across the meadow with that smooth trot which wears down all other four-footed creatures. He was

105

already on the far side of the meadow, and beginning the ascent of the first slope when the glint of the sun on the yellow wild flowers flashed on the eye of Kate. It had all seemed natural until that moment, the only possible thing to do, but now she felt suddenly that Joan was thrown away—thought of the darkness which would soon come—remembered the yellow terror which sometimes gleamed in the eyes of Black Bart after nightfall.

She cried out, but the wolf-dog kept swiftly on his way. She began to run, still calling, but rapidly as she went, Black Bart slid steadily away from her, and when she reached the shoulder of the mountain, she saw the dark form of Bart with the blue patch above it drifting up the wall of the opposite ravine.

She knew where they were going now; it was the old cave upon which she and Dan had come one day in their rides, and Dan had prowled for a long time through the shadowy recesses.

CHAPTER XIX

The Venture

From the moment Joan gave the name of Daddy Dan, the wolf-dog kept to the trail with arrowy straightness. Whatever the limitations of Bart's rather uncanny intelligence, upon one point he was usually letter-perfect, and even when a stranger mentioned Dan in the hearing of the dog it usually brought a whine or at least an anxious look. He hewed to his line now with that animal sense of direction which men can never wholly understand. Boulders and trees slipped away on either side of Joan; now on a descent of the mountain-side he broke into a lope that set the flowers fluttering on her bonnet; now he prowled up the ravine beyond, utterly tireless.

He was strictly business. When she slipped a little from her place as he veered around a rock he did not slow up, as usual, that she might regain her seat, but switched his head back with a growl that warned her into position. That surprise was hardly out of her mind when she saw a gay patch of wild-flowers a little from the line of his direction, and she tugged at his ear to swing him towards it. A sharp jerk of his head tossed her hand aside, and again she caught the glint of wild eyes as he looked back at her. Then she grew grave, puzzled. She trusted Black Bart with all her heart, as only a child can trust dumb animals, but now she sensed a change in him. She had guessed at a difference on that night when Dan came home for the last time; and the same thing seemed to be in the dog to-day.

Before she could make up her mind as to what it might be, Black Bart swung aside up a steep slope, and whisked her into the gloom of a cave. Into the very heart of the darkness he glided and stopped.

"Daddy Dan!" she called.

A faint echo, after a moment, came back to her from the depths of the cave, making her voice strangely deep. Otherwise, there was no answer.

"Bart!" she whispered, suddenly frightened by the last murmur of that echo, "Daddy Dan's not here. Go back!"

She tugged at his ear to turn him, but again that jerk of the head freed his ear. He caught her by the cloak, crouched close to the floor, and she found herself all at once sitting on the gravelly floor of the cave with Bart facing her.

"Bad Bart!" she said, scrambling to her feet.

"Naughty dog!"

She was still afraid to raise her voice in that awful silence, and in the dark. When she glanced around her she made out vague forms through the dimness that might be the uneven walls of the cave, or might be strange and awful forms of night.

"Take me home!"

A growl that went shuddering down the cave stopped her, and now she saw that the eyes of Bart glowed green and yellow. Even then she could not believe that he would harm her, and stretched out a tentative hand. This time she made out the flash of his teeth as he snarled. He was no longer the Bart she had played with around the cabin, but a strange wild thing, and with a scream she darted past him toward the door. Never had those chubby legs flown so fast, but even as the light from the mouth of the cave glimmered around her, she heard a crunching on the gravel from behind, and then a hand, it seemed, caught her cloak and jerked her to a stop.

She fell sprawling, head over heels, and when she looked up, there sat Bart upon his haunches above her, growling terribly, and gripping the end of the cloak. No doubt about it now. Black Bart would have his teeth in her throat if she made another movement toward the entrance. A city child would have either gone mad with terror or else made that fatal struggle to reach the forbidden place, but Joan had learned many things among the mountains, and among others, she knew the difference between the tame and the free. The old dappled cow was tame, for instance; and the Maltese cat, which came too close to Bart the year before and received a broken back for its carelessness, had been tame; and the brown horse with the white face and the dreary eyes was tame. They could be handled, and teased, and petted and bossed about at will. Other creatures were different. For instance, the scream of the hawk always made her shrink a little closer to the ground, or else run helter skelter for the house, and sometimes, up the gulches, she had heard the wailing of a mountain lion on the trail, hunting swiftly, and very hungry. There was even something about the dead eyes of certain lynxes and coyotes and bobcats which Daddy Dan trapped that made Joan feel these animals belonged to a world where the authority of man was only the strength of his hand or his cunning. Not that she phrased these thoughts in definite words, but Joan was very close to nature, and therefore her instincts gave her a weird little touch of wisdom in such matters.

And when she lay there tangled in her cloak and looked up into the glowing eyes of Bart and heard his snarling roll around her, and pass in creepy chills up her back, she nearly died of fear, to be sure, but she lay as still as still, frozen into a part of the rock. Black Bart was gone, and in his place was a terrible creature which belonged there among the shadows, for it could see in the night.

Presently the bright eyes disappeared, and now she saw that Bart lay stretched across the entrance to the cave, where the long shadow was now creeping down the slope. Inches by inches, she ventured to sit up, and all it brought from Bart was a quick turn of the head and a warning growl. It meant as plainly as though he had spoken in so many words: "Stay where you are and I don't care in the least what you do, but don't try to cross this entrance if you fear the length of my teeth and the keenness thereof." And she did fear them, very much, for she remembered the gashes across the back and the terrible rips up the side, of the dead Maltese cat.

She even took a little heart, after a time. A grown-up cannot feel terror or grief as keenly as a child, but neither does terror or grief pass away a tithe as fast. She seemed at liberty to roam about in the cave as long as she did not go near the entrance, and now the shadows and the dimness no longer frightened her. Nothing was terrible except that long, dark body which lay across the entrance to the cave, and she finally got to her feet and began to explore. She came first on a quantity of dead grass heaped in a corner—that was where Satan was stalled, no doubt, and it made all the cave seem almost homelike. She found, too, a number of stones grouped together with ashes in the hollow circle—that was where the fires were built, and there to the side lay the pile of dead wood. A little down the cave and directly in the center of the top, she next saw the natural aperture where the smoke must escape and last of all she came on the bed. Boughs heaped a foot thick with the blankets on top, neatly stretched out, and the tarpaulin over all, made a couch as soft as down and fragrant with the pure scent of evergreens.

Joan tried the surface with a foot that sank to her ankle, then with her hands, and finally sat down to think. The first fear was almost gone; she understood that Bart was keeping her here until Dan came home, and fear does not go hand in hand with understanding. She only wondered, now, at the reason that kept Daddy Dan living in this cave so far from the warm comfort of the cabin, and so far away from her mother; but thinking makes small heads drowsy; and in five minutes Joan lay with her head pillowed on her arm, sound asleep.

When she awoke, the evening-gray of the cave had given place to utter blackness, alarming and thick. Joan sat up with a start; she would have cried out, bewildered, but now she heard a noise on the gravel, and turned to see Daddy Dan entering the cave with Satan behind him, quite distinctly outlined by the sunset outside. Black Bart walked first, looking back over his shoulder as though he led the way.

110

It was partly because the black, silhouetted figures awed her, somewhat, and partly because she wished to give Daddy Dan a gay surprise, that Joan did not run to him. And then, in the darkness, she heard Satan munching the dried grass, and the squeak and rattle as the saddle was drawn off and hung up, scraping against the rock.

"What you been doin', Bart?" queried the voice of Daddy Dan, and the last of Joan's fears fell from her as she listened. "You act kind of worried. If you been runnin' rabbits all day and got your pads full of thorns I'll everlastin'ly treat you rough."

The wolf-dog whined.

"Well, speak up. What you want? Want me over there?"

It would have been a trifle unearthly to most people, but Joan knew the ways of Daddy Dan with Satan and Black Bart. She lay quite still, shivering with pleasure as the footsteps approached her. Then a match scratched—she saw by the blue spurt of flame that he was lighting a pine torch, then whirling it until the flame ate down to the pitchy knot. He held it above his head, and now she saw him plainly: the light cascaded over his shoulders, glowed on his eyes, and then puffed out sidewise in a draught.

Joan was upon her feet, and running toward him with a cry of joy, until she remembered that he was not to be approached like her mother. There were never any bearhugs from him, no caresses, not much laughter. She stopped barely in time, and stood with her fingers interlaced, staring up at him, half delighted, half afraid. She read his mind by microscopic changes in his eyes and lips.

"Munner sent me."

That was wrong, she saw at once.

"And Bart brought me." Much better, now. "And oh, Daddy Dan, I've been *lonesome* for you!"

He continued to stare at her for another moment, and even Joan could not tell whether he was angry or indifferent or pleased.

"Well," he murmured at length, "I guess you're hungry, Joan?"

She knew it was complete acceptance, and she could

hardly keep from a shout of happiness. Daddy Dan had a great aversion to sudden outcries.

"I guess I am," said Joan.

CHAPTER XX

Discipline

He made the preparation for supper with such easy speed that everything seemed to be done by magic hands. When Joan's mother cooked supper there was always much rattling of the stove, then the building of the fire, a long preparation of food, and another interval when things steamed and sizzled on the fire. There followed the setting of the table, and then a long, aching time of hunger when the food was in sight, but one could not eat until Daddy Dan had done this, and Munner had done that. Also, when one did eat, half the taste was taken from things by the necessity of various complicated evolutions of knife and fork. Instance the absurdity of taking the fork under the thumb with the forefinger pressing along the back of the wobbly instrument, when any one could see that the proper, natural way of using a fork was to grasp it daggerwise and drive it firmly through that skidding piece of meat. Not only this, but a cup must be held in one hand, and bread must be broken into little pieces before putting butter on it. Above all, no matter how terribly hard one tried, there was sure to be a mistake, and then a: "Now, Joan, don't do that. This is the way——"

But how different everything was in this delightful house of Daddy Dan!

In an incredibly short time three torches flared about them and filled the air with scents of freshness and the outdoors-scents that went tingling up the nose and filled one with immense possibilities of eating. At the very same time, a few motions caused a heap of wood to catch fire and blaze among the stones while a steady stream of

113

blue-white smoke wavered up toward the top of the cave and disappeared in the shadows. After this her father showed her a little stream of water which must come from a spring far back in the cave, and the current slipped noiselessly along one wall, and dipped out of sight again before it reached the entrance to the place. Here she discovered a little bowl, made out of small stones nicely fitted together, and allowing the water to pour over one edge and out at another with a delicious purling—such crystal clear water that one actually wanted to wash in it even if it was cold, and even if one had the many sore places on fingers and nose and behind the ears.

Behold! no sooner did one turn from the washing of hands and face than the table was miraculously spread upon the surface of a flat rock, with other stones nearby to serve as chairs; and on the table steamed "pone," warmed over; coffee with milk in it—coffee, which was so strictly banned at home!—potatoes sliced to transparent thinness and fried to crisp brown at the edges, and a great slab of meat that fairly shouted to the appetite.

So far so good, but the realization was a thousand fold better than anticipation. No cutting of one's own meat at this enchanted board! The shining knife of Daddy Dan divided it into delectable bits with the speed of light, and it needed only the slighest amount of experimenting and cautious glances to discover that one could use a fork daggerwise, and when in doubt even seize upon a morsel with one's fingers and wipe the fingers afterwards on a bit of the dry grass. One could grasp the cup by both sides, scorning the silly handle, and if occasionally one sipped the coffee with a little noise—which added astonishingly to the taste—there was no sharp warning, no frowning eye to overlook. Besides, at Munner's table, there was never time to pay attention to Joan, for there was talk about vague, abstract things—the price of skins, the melting of the snows, the condition of the passes, the long and troubling argument about the wicker chairs, with some remarkably foolish asides, now and then, concerning happiness and love—when all the time any one with half an eye could see that the thing to do was to

114

eat and eat and eat until that hollow place ceased to be. Talking came afterwards.

In the house of Daddy Dan all these things were ordered as they should be. Not a word was said; not a glance of criticism rested upon her; when her tin plate was cleared she heard no reproofs for eating too greedily, but she was furnished anew from the store of good things on the rock.

In place of conversation, there were other matters to occupy the mind during the meal. For presently she observed the beautiful head of Satan just behind his master —Satan, who could pass over noisy gravel with the softness of a cat, and now loomed out of the deeper night down the cavern. Inch by inch, with infinite caution and keenly pricked ears, the head lowered beside Dan, and the quivering, delicate muzzle stole towards a fragment of the "pone." Joan watched breathlessly and then she saw that in spite of the caution of that movement her father knew all about it—just a glint of amusement in the corner of his eyes, just a slight twitch at the corners of his mouth to tell Joan that he was as delighted as a boy playing a trick. Barely in time to save the morsel of pone, he spoke and the head was dashed up. Yet Satan was not entirely discouraged. If he could not steal the bread he would beg for it. It made Joan pause in her destruction of the edibles, not to watch openly, for an instinct told her that the thing to do was to note these by-plays from the corner of one's eye, as Daddy Dan did, and swallow the ripples of mirth that came tickling in the throat. She knew perfectly well that Satan would have it in the end, for of all living things not even Munner had such power over Dan as the black stallion. He maneuvered adroitly. First he circled the table and stood opposite the master, begging with his eyes, but Dan looked fixedly down at the rock until an impatient whinny called up his eyes. Then he pretended the most absolute surprise.

"Why, Satan, you old scoundrel, what are you doin' over there? Get back where you belong?"

He gestured with a thumb over his shoulder and Satan glided around the rock and stood once more behind Dan.

"Manners?" continued Dan. "You ain't got 'em. You'll

be tryin' to sit down at the table with me, pretty soon." He concluded: "But I'll teach you one of these days, and you'll smart for a week."

Even at the mock menace Joan trembled a little, but to her astonishment Satan paid not the slightest heed. Dan sat with his hat on his head—which was a new and delightful event at the table—and now the stallion took the hat by the crown, dexterously, and raised it just an inch and put it back in place. Black Bart, having crept out of the shadows sat down near Joan with his long red tongue lolling out. This procedure called a growl from him, but the master continued eating without the slightest interest, apparently, in Satan's insolence.

A velvety muzzle appeared, with the chin resting on the shoulder of Dan and the great, luminous eyes above. He whinnied so softly that it was not more than a human whisper, and meant almost as much.

"Oh," said Dan, in all seeming just roused to attention, "hungry, old boy?"

He raised the morsel of "pone" between thumb and forefinger, holding it tightly. Then it was a joy to watch Satan. He tried to tug it all away at once, but only a fragment broke off. He stamped in impatience, and then went to work to nibble the bread away on all sides of Dan's fingers, very fine work for such broad, keen chisels as Satan's teeth, but he went about it with the skill of long practice, turning his head this way and that and always watching the face of the master with sidewise eyes, one ear forward and one ear back. Finally the tight fingers opened out, and Satan gathered the last crumbs from the smooth palm.

Two or three times during this performance Black Bart had half risen from his haunches and a growl swelled almost inaudibly in his throat, but now he stalked around the table and pushed his narrow head between Dan's shoulder and the stallion. A snarl of incredible ferocity made Satan turn, but without the slightest dread, apparently. For an instant the two stood nose to nose, Black Bart a picture of snarling danger and Satan with curiously pricking ears and bright eyes. The growling rose towards a crescendo, a terrible sound; then a lean hand shot out

116

with that speed which Joan could never comprehend—and which always made her think, rather breathlessly, of the strike of a snake. The fingers settled around the muzzle of Bart.

"Of all the no-good houn'-dogs," declared Dad, "you're the worst, and the most jealousest. Lie down!"

Bart obeyed, slowly, but his evil eyes were fixed upwards upon the head of Satan.

"If you got any manners," remarked Dan, "you'll be sayin' that you're sorry."

The ears flattened along the snaky head; otherwise no answer.

"Sorry!" repeated the master.

Out of the deep throat of Black Bart, infinitely ludicrously small, came a whine which was more dog-like than anything Joan had ever heard, before, from the wolf.

"Now," continued the implacable master, "you go over in that corner, and lie down."

Black Bart arose with a finally ugly look for Satan and sneaked with hanging head and tail to the outer edge of the circle of light.

"Farther! Clear over there in the dark," came the order, and Bart had to uncoil himself again in the very act of lying down and retreat with another ominous growl clear into the darkness. Satan held his head high and watched triumphantly.

But Joan felt that this was a little hard on Bart; she wanted to run over and comfort him but she knew from of old that it was dangerous to interfere where Daddy Dan was disciplining either horse or wolf; besides, she was not quite free from her new awe for Bart.

"All right," said the master presently, and without raising his voice.

It brought a dark thunderbolt rushing into the circle of the light and stopping at Dan's side with such suddenness that his paws slid in the gravel. There he stood, actually wagging his bushy tail—an unprecedented outburst of joy for Bart!—and staring hungrily into the face of Dan. She saw a wonderful softening in the eyes of her father as he looked at the great, dangerous beast.

117

"You ain't a bad sort," he said, "but you need puttin' in place continual."

Black Bart whined agreement.

After that, when the dishes were being cleared away and cleaned with a speed fully as marvelous as the preparation of the supper, Joan remembered with a guilty start the message which she should have given to Daddy Dan, and she brought out the paper, much rumpled.

He stood by the fire to read the letter.

"Dan come back to us. The house is empty and there's no sign of you except your clothes and the skins you left drying in the vacant room. Joan sits all day mourning for you, and my heart is breaking. Oh, Dan, I don't grieve so much for what has been done, but I tremble for what you may do in the future."

With the letter still in his hand Dan walked thoughtfully to Satan and took the fine head between his fingers

"S'pose some gent was to drop you, Satan," he murmured. "S'pose he was to plug you while you was doin' your best to take me where I want to go. S'pose he shot you not for anything you'd done but because of something agin me. And s'pose after killin' you he was to sneak up on me with a lot of other gents and try to murder me before I had a chance to fight back. Satan, wouldn't I be right to trail 'em all—and kill 'em one by one? Wouldn't I?"

Joan heard very little of the words—only a soft murmur of anxiety, and she saw that Daddy Dan was very thoughtful indeed. The stallion reached for the brim of Dan's hat —it was withdrawn from his reach—his head bowed, like a nod of assent.

"Why, even Satan can see I'm right," murmured Dan, and moving back to the fire, he tore the letter into many pieces which fluttered down in a white stream and made the blaze leap up.

118

CHAPTER XXI

The Acid Test

Mrs. Johnny Sommers managed to preserve her dignity while she escorted the visitor into the front room, and even while she asked him to sit down and wait, but once she had closed the door behind her she cast dignity far away and did two steps at a time going upstairs. The result was that she reached the room of Betty Neal entirely out of breath: two hundred pounds of fat, good-natured widowhood do not go with speed. She tossed open the door without any preliminary knock and stood there very red with a clearly defined circle of white in the center of each cheek. For a moment there was no sound except her panting and Betty Neal stared wildly at her from above her book.

"He's come!" gasped Mrs. Sommers.

"Who?"

"Him!"

As if this odd explanation made everything clear, Betty Neal sprang from her chair and she grew so pale that every freckle stood out.

"Him!" she echoed ungrammatically.

Then: "Where is he? Let me downstairs!"

But the widow closed the door swiftly behind her and leaned her comfortable bulk against it.

"You ain't goin'," she asserted. "You ain't goin', least-ways not till you got time to think it over."

"I haven't time to think. I——he——"

"That was the way with me," nodded Mrs. Sommers, and her eyes were tragic. "I went ahead and married Johnny in spite of everything, and look at me now—a widder! No, I ain't sorry for myself because I was a fool."

119

"Mrs. Sommers," said Betty, "will you please step out of my way?"

"Honey, for heaven's sake think a minute before you go down and face that man. He's dangerous. When I opened the door and seen him, I tell you the shivers went up my back."

"Is he thin? Is he pale?" cried Betty Neal. "How did he get away? Did he escape? Did they parole him? Did they pardon him? Did he——"

"Let me get down!" she cried.

Mrs. Sommers flung away from the door.

"Then go and marry your—man-killer!"

But Betty Neal was already clattering down the stairs. Half way to the bottom her strength and courage ebbed suddenly from her; she went on with short steps, and when at last she closed the parlor door behind her, she was staring as if she looked at a ghost.

Yet Vic Gregg was not greatly changed—a little thinner perhaps, and just now he certainly did not have his usual color. The moment she appeared he jumped to his feet as if he had heard a shot, and now he stood with his feet braced a little to meet a shock, one hand twitching and playing nervously with the embroidered cloth on the table. She did not speak: merely stood with her fingers still gripping the handle of the door as if she were ready to dart away at the first alarm. A wave of pain went over the face of Vic Gregg and remained looking at her out of his eyes, for all that his single-track, concentrated mind could perceive in her was the thing he took for fear.

"Miss Neal," he said. His voice shook, straightened out again. He made her think of one of her big school boys who had forgotten his lesson and now stood cudgeling his memory and dreading that terrible nightmare of "staying after school!" She had a wild desire to laugh.

"Miss Neal, I ain't here to try to take up things that can't be took up ag'in." Apparently he had prepared the speech carefully, and now he went on with more ease: "I'm leavin' these here parts for some place unknown. Before I go I jest want to say I know I was wrong from the beginnin'. All I want to say is that I was jest all sort

120

of tied up in a knot inside and when I seen you with——
him——" He stopped. "I hope you marry some gent
that's worth you, only they ain't any such. An'—I want
to wish you good-luck, an' say good-by."

He swept the perspiration from his forehead, and
caught up his hat; he had been through the seventh circle
of torture.

"Oh, Vic, dear!" cried a voice he <u>had</u> never heard before. Then a flurry of skirts, then arms about him, then
tears and laughter, and eyes which went hungrily over
his face.

"I been a houn'-dog. My God, Betty, you don't mean
——"

"That I love you, Vic. I never knew what it was to love
you before."

"After I been a man-killin', lyin', sneakin'——"

"Don't you say another word. Vic, it was all my fault."

"It wasn't. It was mine. But if you'd only kind of held
off a little and gone easy with me——"

"You didn't give me a chance."

"When I looked back from the road you wasn't standin'
in the door."

"I was. And you didn't look back."

"I did."

"Vic Gregg, are you trying to——"

But the anger fled from her as suddenly as it had come.

"I don't care. I'll take all the blame."

"I don't want you to. I won't let you."

She laughed hysterically.

"Vic, tell me that you're free?"

"I'm paroled."

"Thank God! Oh, I've prayed and prayed—Vic, don't
talk. Sit down there—so! I just want to look and look at
you. There's a hollow, hungry place in me that's filling up
again."

"It was Pete Glass," said Gregg brokenly. "He—he
trusted me clean through when the rest was lookin' at me
like I was a snake. Pete got word to the governor, and
so——"

There followed a long interval of talk that meant nothing, and then, as the afternoon waned towards evening,

121

and the evening towards dark, he told her the whole story of the long adventure. He left out nothing, not a detail that might tell against him. When he came to the moment when Glass persuaded him to go back and betray Barry he winced, but set his jaw and plunged ahead. She, too, paled when she heard that, and for a moment she had to cover her eyes, but she was older by half a life-time than she had been when he was last with her, and now she read below the surface. Besides, Vic had offered to undo what he had done, had offered to stay and fight for Barry, and surely that evened the score!

There was a light rap on the door, and then Mrs. Sommers came in with a tray.

"Maybe you young folks forgot about supper," she said. "I just thought I'd bring in a bite for you."

She placed it on the table, and then lingered, delighted, while her eyes went over them together and one by one. Perhaps Betty Neal was a fool for throwing herself away on a gun-fighter, but at least Mrs. Sommers was furnished with a story which half Alder would know by to-morrow. The walls of her house were not sound proof. Besides, Mrs. Sommers had remarkably keen ears.

"They's been a gentleman here askin' for you, Vic," she said, "but I thought maybe you wouldn't like it much to be disturbed. So I told him you wasn't here."

Her smile fairly glowed with triumph.

"Thanks," said Gregg, "but who was he?"

"I never seen him before. Anyway, it didn't much matter. He wanted to see some of the rest of the boys quite bad: Pete Glass and Ronicky Joe, and Sliver Waldron, and Gus Reeve. He seemed to want to see 'em all particular bad."

"Pete Glass and Ronicky and—the posse!" murmured Vic. He grew thoughtful. "He wanted to see me, too?"

"Very particular, and he seemed kind of down-hearted when he found that Pete was out of town. Wanted to know when he might be back."

"What sort of a lookin' gent was he?" asked Vic, and his voice was sharp.

"Him? Oh, he looked like a tenderfoot to me. Terrible polite, though, and he had a voice that wasn't hardly rougher'n a girl's. Seemed like he was sort of embarrassed just talkin' to me." She smiled at the thought, but Gregg was on his feet now, his hands on the shoulders of Mrs. Sommers as though he would try to shake information from her loose bulk.

"Look quick, now," he said. "Where did you send him?"

"How you talk! Why, where should I send him? I told him like as not Ronicky and Sliver and Gus would be down to Lorrimer's——"

The groan of Vic made her stop with a gasp.

"What did he look like?"

Mrs. Sommers was very sober. Her smile congealed. "Black hair, and young, and good-lookin', and b-b-brown eyes, and——"

"God!"

"Vic," cried Betty Neal, "what is it!" She looked around her in terror.

"It's Barry."

He turned towards the door, and then stopped, in an agony of indecision. Betty Neal was before him, blocking the way with her arms outstretched.

"Vic, you shan't go. You shan't go. You've told me yourself that he's sure death."

"God knows he is."

"You won't go, Vic?"

"But the others! Ronicky—Gus——"

She stammered in her fear.

"That's their lookout! They're three to one. Let them kill——"

"But they don't know him. They've never been close enough to see his face. Besides, no three men—I—he—for God's sake tell me what to do!"

"Stay here—if you love me. I won't let you go. I won't."

"I got to warn them."

"You'll be killed!"

He tore away her hands.

"I got to warn them—but who'll I help? Them three against Dan? He saved me—twice! But—I got to go!"

"If you fight for him first he'll only turn on you after-wards. Vic, stay here."

"What good's my life? What good's it if I'm a yaller dog ag'in? I'm goin' out—and be a man!"

CHAPTER XXII

The Fifth Man

The moment Vic Gregg stood in the open air, with the last appeal of Betty ringing still at his ear, he felt a profound conviction that he was about to die and he stood a moment breathing deeply, taking the faint alkali scent of the dust and looking up to the start. It was that moment when night blends with day and there is no sign of light in the sky except that the stars burn more and more bright as the darkness thickens, and Vic Gregg watched the stars draw down more closely and believed that he was seeing this for the last time. Alder seemed inexpressibly dear to him as he stood there through a little space, and the vaguely discernible outlines of the shacks along the street were like the faces of friends. In that house behind him was Betty Neal, waiting, praying for him, and indeed, had it not been for shame, he would have weakened now and turned back. For he hardly knew which way to turn. He wanted to save Ronicky and the other two from the attack of Barry, yet he would not lay a trap for Dan. To Barry he owed a vast debt; his debt to the three was that which any human being owes to another. He had to save them from the wolf which ran through the night in the body of a man.

That thought sent him at a run for Captain Lorrimer's saloon. It was lighted brilliantly by the gasoline lamp within, but a short distance away from it he heard no sound and his imagination drew a terrible picture of the big, empty room, with three dead men lying in the center of it where the destroyer had reached them one by one. That was what took the blood from his face and made him a white mask of tragedy when he stepped into the door of the saloon. It was quiet, but half a dozen men sat at the tables in the corner, and among them were Ronicky and the other two. Sliver Waldron was in the very act of pulling back his chair and perhaps all three had just come in. Perhaps Barry had come here to look for his quarry and found them not yet arrived; perhaps he was now hunting in other places through the town; perhaps he was even now crouched in the shadow near at hand and ready to attack.

It made the hand of Vic Gregg contract with a cruel pressure when it fell on the shoulder of Sliver Waldron.

"Now, what in hell!" grunted that hardened warrior.

He had no love for Vic Gregg since that day when the posse rode through the hills after him; neither had Ronicky or Gus Reeve, who rose from their chairs as if at a signal.

"Come with me, gents," said Vic. "An' come quick!"

They asked no questions and did not stay to argue the point for he had that in his face which meant action. He led them outside, and behind the horse shed of the saloon.

"We're alone?" he asked.

"Nothin' in sight."

"Look sharp."

They peered about them through the night, and a wan moon only helped to make the darkness visible.

"Gents, we may be alone now, but we ain't goin' to be alone long. Get your hosses and ride like hell. Barry is in town!"

"Vic, you're drunk."

"I tell you, he's been seen!"

"Then by God," growled Sliver Waldron, "lead me to him. I need to have a little talk with that gent."

"Lead you *to* him?" echoed Vic Gregg. "Sliver, are you hungerin' to push daisies?"

"Look here, Bud," answered the older man, and he laid a hand on the shoulder of Vic. "You been with this Barry gent, and you've lived in his house. D'you mean to say you're one of the lot that talks about him like he was a ghost bullets couldn't harm? I tell you, son, they's been so much chatter about him that folks forget he's human. I'm goin' to remind 'em of that little fact."

126

Vic Gregg groaned. Even while he talked he was glancing over his shoulder as if he feared the shadows under the moon. Hiis voice was half gasp, half whisper.

"Sliver—Ronicky—don't ask me how I know—jest believe me when I say Dan Barry'll never die by the hand of any man. I tell you—he can see in the dark!"

A soft oath from Gus Reeve; a twitching of Ronicky's head told that this last had taken effect. Sliver Waldron suddenly altered his manner.

"All right, Vic. Trot back into town, or come with us. We're going to move out."

"The wisest thing you ever done, Sliver."

"I'm feelin' the same way," breathed Gus Reeve.

"S'long," whispered Vic Gregg, and faded into the night, running.

The others, without a word among themselves, gathered their horses and struck down the valley out of Alder. The padding and swish of the sand about the feet of their mounts; the very creaking of the saddle leather seemed to alarm them, and they were continually turning and looking back. That is, Gus Reeve and Ronicky Joe manifested these signs of trouble, but Sliver Waldron, riding in the center of the trio, never moved his head. They were hardly well out of the town when a swift rush of hoof beats swept up from behind, and a horseman darted into the pale mist of the valley bending low over his pommel to cut the wind of his riding.

"Who is it?"

"Vic Gregg!" muttered Gus Reeve. "Stir along, Sliver. Vic ain't lingerin' any!"

But Sliver Waldron drew rein, and let his horse go on at a walk.

"Hearin' you talk, Ronicky," he said, "you'd think you was really scared of Dan Barry."

Ronicky Joe stiffened in his saddle and peered through the uncertain light to make out if Sliver were jesting. But the latter seemed perfectly grave.

"A gent would almost think," went on Sliver, "that we three was runnin' away from Barry, instead of goin' out to set a trap for him."

There was something nearly akin to a grunt from Gus

127

Reeve, but Ronicky merely continued to stare at the leader.

" 'S-a matter of fact," said Sliver, "when Vic was talkin' I sort of felt the chills go up my back. How about you, Ronicky?"

"I'll tell a man," sighed Ronicky. "While Vic was talkin' I seen that devil comin' on his hoss like he done when he broke out of the cabin that night. I'll tell you straight, Sliver. I had my gun drilled on him. I couldn't of missed; but after I fired he kept straight on. It was like puncturin' a shadow!"

"Sure," nodded Sliver. "Shootin' by night ain't ever a sure thing."

Ronicky wiped his heated brow.

"So I sent Vic away before he had a chance to get real nervous. But when he comes back—well boys, it'll be kind of amusin' to watch Vic's face when he saunters into town tomorrow and sees Dan Barry—maybe dead, maybe in the irons. Eh?"

Only a deep silence answered him, but in the interest which his words excited the terror seemed to have left Ronicky and Gus. They rode close, their heads toward Sliver alone.

"There goes Vic," mused Sliver. "There he goes—go on. Mac, you old fool!—scared to death ridin' for his life. And why? Because he believes some ghost stories he's heard about Dan Barry!"

"Ghost stories?" echoed Reeve. "Some of 'em ain't fairy tales, Sliver."

"Jest name one that ain't!"

"Well, the way he trailed Jim Silent. We've all heard of Silent, and Barry was too good for him."

"Bah," sneered Sliver. "Too good for Silent? Ye lied readily enough: Booze done for Silent long before Barry come along."

"That right?"

"I'll tell a man it is. Mind you, I don't say Barry ain't handy with his gun; but he's done a little and the gents have furnished the trimmin's. Look here, if Barry is the man-eater they say, why did he pick a time for comin' down when the sheriff was out of town?"

"By God!" exclaimed Ronicky. "I never thought of that!"

"Sure you didn't," chuckled Sliver. "But this sucker figures that you and Gus and me will be easy pickin's. He figures we'll do what Vic did—hit for the tall pines. Then he'll blow around how he ran the four of us out of Alder. Be pleasant comin' back to talk like that, eh?"

There was a volley of rapid curses from the other two.

"We'll get this cheap skate, Sliver," suggested Ronicky. We'll get this ghost and tie him up and take him back to Alder and make a show of him."

"We will," nodded Sliver. "Have you figured how?"

"Lie out here in the bush. He'll hunt around Alder all night and when the mornin' comes he'll leave and he'll come out this way. We'll be ready for him where the valley's narrow down there. They say his hoss and his dog is as bad as any two ordinary men. Well, that's three of them and here's three of us. It's an even break, eh?"

"Ronicky," murmured Sliver, "I always knowed you had the brains. We'll take this gent and tame him, and run him back to Alder on the end of a rope."

Gus Reeve whooped and waved his hat at the thought.

So the three reached the point where the shadowy walls of the valley narrowed, drew almost together. There they placed the horses in a hollow near the southern cliff, and they returned to take post. There was only one bridle path which wound through the gulch here, and the three concealed themselves behind a thicket of sagebrush to wait.

They laid their plan carefully. Each man was to have his peculiar duty: Gus Reeve, an adept with the rope, would wait until the black stallion was cantering past and then toss his noose and throw the horse. At the same instant, Ronicky Joe would shoot the wolf-dog, and Sliver Waldron would perforate Dan Barry while the latter rolled in the dust, unless, indeed, he was pinioned by the fall of his horse, in which case they would have the added glory of taking him alive.

By the time all these details were settled the pale moonlight was shot through with the rose of dawn. Then, rapidly, the mountains lifted into view, range beyond range, all their gulleys deep blue and purple, and here and there sharp triangles of snow. There was not a cloud, not a trace of mist, and through the crisp, thin air the vision carried as if through a telescope. They could count the trees on the upper ridges; and that while the floor of the valley was still in shadow. This in turn grew brilliant, and everywhere the sage brush glittered like foliage carved in gray-green quartz.

It was then that they saw Dan Barry, while the dawn was still around them, and before the sun pushed up in the east above the mountains. He came winding down the bridle path with the dawn glittering on the side of Satan, and a dark, swift form spiriting on ahead.

"Look at him!" muttered Sliver Waldron. "The damned wolf is a scout. See him nose around that hummock? Watch him smell behind that bush. The black devil!"

Bart, in fact, wove a loose course before his master, running here and there to all points of vantage, as if he knew that danger lurked ahead, but where he came close, with only the narrow passage between the cliffs, he seemed to make up his animal brain that there could be no trouble in so constricted a place, and darted straight ahead.

"They're ours," whispered Waldron. "Steady, boys. Gus, get your rope, get ready!"

Gus tossed the noose a little wider, and gathered himself for the throw, but it seemed as if the wolf saw or heard the movement. He stopped suddenly and stood with his head high; behind him the rider checked the black horse; all three waited.

"He's tryin' to get the wind," chuckled Waldron, "but the wind is ag'in' our faces!"

It was only a slight breeze, but it came directly against the lurking three; and moreover the scent of the sage was particularly keen at this time of the day, and quite sufficient to blur the scent of man even in the keen nostrils of Black Bart. Only for a second or so he stood there sniffing the wind, a huge animal, larger than any wolf the three had ever seen; his face wise in a certain bear-like fashion from the three gray marks in the center of his forehead. Now he trotted ahead, and the stallion broke into a gallop behind.

"My God," whispered Sliver to Gus, "don't spoil that hoss when you daub the rope on him! Look at that action; like runnin' water!"

They came more rapidly. As if the rider knew that a point of danger was there to be passed, he spoke to his mount, and Satan lengthened into a racing gait that blew the brim of the rider's hat straight up. On they came. The wolf-dog darted past. Then as the horse swept by, Gus Reeve rose from behind his bush and the rope darted snakelike from his hand. The forefeet of Satan landed in the noose, and the next instant the back flung weight of Gus tightened the rope, and Satan shot over upon his side, flinging the master clear of the saddle.

It sent him rolling over and over in the dust, and Sliver Waldron was on his feet with both guns in action, sending bullet after bullet towards the tumbling body. Gus Reeve was running towards the stallion, his rope in action to entangle one of the hind-feet and make sure of his prey; Ronicky Joe had leaped up with a yell and blazed away at Black Bart.

It was no easy mark to strike, for the moment the rope shot out from the hand of Gus, the wolf-dog whirled in his tracks and darted straight for the scene of action. It was that, perhaps, which troubled the aim of Ronicky more than anything else, for wild animals do not whirl in this fashion and run for an assailant. He had expected to find himself plugging away at a flying target in the distance; instead, the black monster was rushing straight for him, silently. Indeed, all that followed was in silence after that first wild Indian yell from Ronicky Joe. His gun barked, but Black Bart was running like a football player down a broken field, swerving here and there with uncanny speed. Again, again, Joe missed, and then flung up his arm to ward the flying danger. But Black Bart shot from the ground to make his kill. He could bring down the strongest bull in the herd. What was the arm of a man to him? His snake-like head shot through that futile guard; his teeth cut off the screams of Ronicky Joe. Down they went. The gun flew from the hand of Ronicky; for an instant he struggled with hands and writhing legs, and then the murderous teeth of Bart sank deeper, found the life. The dead body was limp, but Bart, shaking his hold deeper to make sure, glared across to the fallen master.

The third man had died for Grey Molly.

All this had happened in a second, and the body of Barry was still rolling when a gun flashed in his hand, drawn while he tumbled. It spat fire and Sliver Waldron staggered forward drunkenly, waved both his armed hands as if he were trying to talk by signal, and pitched on his face into the dust.

The fourth man had died for Grey Molly.

No gun was destined for Gus Reeve, however. Black Bart had left the lifeless body of his victim and was darting towards the third man; the master was on his knee, raising his gun for the last shot; but Gus Reeve was blind to all that had happened. He saw only the black stallion, the matchless prize of horseflesh. He tossed a loop in the taut rope to entangle a hind foot, but that slackening of the line gave Satan his instant's purchase, and a moment later he was on his feet, whirled, and two iron-hard hoofs crushed the whole framework of the man's chest like an egg-shell. The impact lifted him from his feet, but before that body struck the ground the life was fled from it.

The fifth man had died for Grey Molly.

CHAPTER XXIII

Bad News

News of the Killing at Alder, as they call that night's slaughter to this day in the mountain-desert traveled swiftly, and lost nothing of bulk and burden on the way; so that two days later, when Lee Haines went down for mail to the wretched little village in the valley, he heard the store-keeper retailing the story to an awe-stricken group. How the tale had crossed all the wild mountains which lay between in so brief a space no man could say, but first there ran a whisper and then a stir, and then half a dozen men came in at once, each with an elaboration of the theme more horrible than the last. The store-keeper culled the choicest fragments from every version, strung them together with a narrative of his own fertile invention, polished off the tale by a few rehearsals in his home, and then placed his product on the open market. The very first day he kept the store-room well filled from dawn until dark.

And this was the creation to which Lee Haines had to listen, impatient, sifting the chaff from the grains of truth. Down upon Alder, exactly at midnight, had ridden a cavalcade headed by that notorious, half-legendary man-slayer, Dan Barry—Whistling Dan. While his crew of two-score hardened ruffians held the doors and the windows with leveled rifles, Barry had entered with a gun and a wolf—a wild wolf, and had butchered ten men, wantonly. To add to the mystery, there was no motive of robbery for the crime. One sweeping visitation of death, and then the night-riders had rushed away. Nor was this all, for Sheriff Pete Glass, hearing of the tragedy, had ridden to Rickett, the county seat, and from this strategic point of vantage he was sending out a call for the most practiced fighters on the mountain-desert. He wanted twenty men proved beyond the shadow of question for courage, endurance, speed, and surety in action.

"And," concluded the store-keeper, fixing his eye upon Lee Haines, "if you want a long ride free of charge, and ten bucks a day with chow thrown in—some of you gents ought to go to Rickett and chin with Pete."

Haines waited to hear no more. He even forgot to ask for the Barry mail, swung into his saddle, and rode with red spurs back to the cabin in the mountains. There he drew Buck Daniels aside, and they walked among the rocks while Haines told his story. When it was ended they sat on adjoining boulders and chucked pebbles aimlessly into the emptiness beyond the cliff.

"Maybe," said Buck suddenly, "it wasn't Dan at all. He sure wouldn't be ridin' with no crowd of gents like that."

"A fool like that store-keeper could make a crowd of Indians out of one papoose," answered Haines. "It was Dan. Who else would be traipsing around with a dog that looks like a wolf—and hunts men?"

"I remember when Dan cornered Jim Silent in that cabin, and all Jim's gang was with him. Black Bart——"

"Buck," cut in Haines, "you've remembered plenty."

After a moment: "When are you going in to break the news to Kate?"

Buck Daniels regarded him with angry astonishment.

"Me?" he cried. "I'd sooner cut my tongue out!" He drew a great breath. "I feel like—like Dan was dead!"

"The best thing for Kate if he were."

"That's a queer thing to say, Lee. The meat would be rotted off your bones six years ago in Elkhead if it hadn't been for Whistlin' Dan."

"I know it, Buck. But I'll tell you straight that I could never feel towards Dan as if he were a human being, but a wolf in the hide of a man. He turned my blood cold; he always has."

Buck Daniels groaned aloud as thoughts poured back on him.

"Of all the pals that ever a man had," he said sadly,

"there never was a partner like Whistlin' Dan. There was never another gent that would go through hell for you jest because you'd eaten meat with him. The first time I met him I tried to double-cross him, because I had my orders from Silent. And Dan played clean with me—by God, he shook hands with me when he left."

He straightened a little.

"So help me God, Lee, I've never done a crooked thing more since I shook hands with Dan that day." He sat silent, but breathing hard. "Well, this is the end of Whistlin' Dan. The law will never let up on him now; but I tell you, Haines, I'm sick inside and I'd give my right hand plumb to the wrist to set him straight and bring him back to Kate. Go in and tell her, Lee. I—I'll wait for you here."

"You'll be damned," cried Haines. "I've done my share by bringing the word this far. You can relay it."

Buck Daniels produced a silver dollar.

"Heads or tails?"

"Heads!" said Haines.

The dollar spun upwards, winking, and clanked on the rocks, tails up. Haines stared at it with a grisly face.

"Good God," he muttered, "what'll I do, Buck, if she faints?"

"Faints?" echoed Daniels, "there's no fear of that! The first thing you'll have to do is to saddle her horse."

"Now, what in hell are you driving at?"

"She'll be thinkin' of Joan. God knows she worried enough because Dan hasn't brought the kid back before this, but when she hears what he's done now, she'll know that he's wild for keeps and she'll be on the trail to bring the young un home."

He turned his back cleanly on the house and set his shoulders tense.

"Go on, Lee. Be a man."

He heard the steps of Haines start briskly enough for the house, but they trailed away, slowly and more slowly, and finally there was a long pause.

"He's standing at the door," muttered Buck. "Thank God I ain't in his boots."

He jerked out his papers and tobacco, but in the very

135

act of twisting the cigarette tight the door slammed and he ripped the flimsy thing in two. He started to take another paper, but his fingers were so unsteady that he could not pull away the single sheet of tissue which he wanted. Then his hands froze in place.

A faint tapping came out to him.

"He—he's rapping on her door," whispered Buck, and remained fixed in place, his eyes staring straight before him.

The seconds slipped away.

"He's turned yaller," murmured Buck. "He couldn't do it. It'll be up to me!"

But he had hardly spoken the words when a low cry came out to him from the house. Then the silence again, but Buck Daniels began to mop his forehead.

After that, once, twice, and again he made the effort to turn towards the house, but when he finally succeeded it was whole minutes later, and Lee Haines was leading a saddled horse from the coral. Kate stood beside the cabin, waiting.

When he reached her, she was already mounted. He halted beside her, panting, his hand on her bridle.

"Don't do it, Kate!" he pleaded. "Lemme go with you. Lemme go and try to help."

The brisk wind up the gulch set her clothes fluttering, stirred the hair about the rim of her hat, and she seemed to Buck more gracefully, more beautifully young than he had ever seen her; but her face was like stone.

"You'd be no help," she answered. "When I get to the place I may have to meet—him! Would you face him, Buck?"

His hand fell away from the bridle. It was not so much what she said as the cold, steady voice with which she spoke that unnerved him. Then, without a farewell, she turned the brown horse around and struck across the meadow at a swift gallop. Buck turned to meet the sick face of Haines.

"Let me have that flask."

Buck produced a metal "life-saver," and Haines with nervous hands unscrewed the top and lifted it to his

136

lips. He lowered it after a long moment and stood bracing himself against the wall.

"It was hell, Buck. God help me if I ever have to go through a thing like that again."

"I see what you done," said Buck angrily. "You walked right in and took your story in both hands and knocked her down with it. Haines, of all the ornery, thick-headed cayuses I ever see, you're the most out-beatin'est!"

"I couldn't help it."

"Why not?"

"When I went in she took one look at me and then jumped up and stood as straight as a pine tree.

" 'Lee,' she said, 'what have you heard?' "

" 'About what?' I asked her, and I looked sort of indifferent."

"Bah!" snorted Buck. "She could see death an' hell written all over your face, most like."

"I suppose," muttered Haines, "I—I was sick!

" 'Tell me!' she said, comin close up.

" 'He's gone wild again,' was all I could put my tongue to.

"Then I blurted it out. I had to get rid of the damned story some way, and the quickest way seemed the best—how Dan rode into Alder and did the killing.

"When I got to that she gave one cry."

"I know," said Buck, shuddering. "Like something dying."

"Then she asked me to saddle her horse. I begged her to let me go with her, and she said to me what she just now said to you. And so I stayed. What good could we do against that devil?"

CHAPTER XXIV

The Music

To the last ravine Kate's horse carried her easily enough, but that mountain pass was impenetrable through all its length to anything except the uncanny agility of Satan, and so she left the cow-pony in the bottom of the gorge and climbed the last rise on foot.

On the mountainside above her, it was not easy to locate the cave, for the slope was clawed into ravines and confused with meaningless criss-cross gulches. Whatever scrub evergreens grew there stood under the shade of boulders which threatened each instant to topple over and go thundering to the base. She had come upon the cave by chance in her ride with Dan, and now she hunted vainly through the great stones for the entrance. A fresh wind, chill with the snows of the upper peaks, pulled and tugged at her and cut her face and hands with flying bits of sand. It kept up a whistling so insistent that it was some time before she recognized in the hum of the gale a different note, not of pleasant music, but a thin, shrill sound that blended with the voice of the wind.

The instant she heard it she stopped short on the lee-side of a tall rock and looked about her in terror. The mountains walked away on every side, and those resolute masses gave her courage. She listened, for the big rock cut away the breath of the wind about her ears and she could make out the whistling more clearly. It was a strain as delicate as a pin point ray of light in a dark room, but it made Kate tremble.

Until the sound ended she stayed there by the rock, hearkening, but the moment it ceased she gathered her resolution with a great effort and went straight toward the source of the whistling. It was only a moment away, although the wind had made it seem much farther, and she came on the tall, narrow opening with Joan sitting on a rock just within. Instead of the blue cloak, she was wrapped in a tawny hide, and the yellow hair blew this way and that, unsheltered from the wind. The loneliness of the little figure made Kate's heart ache, made her pause on her way, and while she hesitated, Joan's head rested back against the rock, her eyes half closed, her lips pursed, she began to whistle that same keen, eerie music.

It brought Kate to her in a rush.

"Oh Joan!" she cried. "My baby!"

And she would have swept the child into her arms, but Joan slipped out from under her very fingers and stood a little distance off with her hands pressed against the wall on either side of her, ready to dart one way or the other. It was not sudden terror, but rather a resolute determination to struggle against capture to the end, and her blue eyes were blazing with excitement. Kate was on her knees with her arms held out.

"Joan, dear, have you forgotten munner?"

The wildness flickered away from the eyes of the child little by little.

"Munner?" she repeated dubiously.

No shout of welcome, no sudden rush, no arms to fling about her mother. But if her throat was dry and closed Kate allowed no sign of it to creep into her voice.

"Where's Daddy Dan?"

"He's gone away."

"Where?"

"Oh—over there!"

The mother rose slowly to her feet, and looked out across the mountains as if in search of aid. For her mind had harked back to that story her father used to tell of the coming of Dan Barry; how he had ridden across the hills one evening and saw, walking against the sunset, a tattered boy who whistled strangely as he went, and when old Joe Cumberland asked where he was going he had only waved a vague hand toward the north and answered, "Oh—over there. It was sufficient destination for him, it was sufficient explanation now for the child. She remembered how she, herself a child then, had sat at her father's table and watched the brown face of the strange boy with fascination, and the wild, quick eyes which went everywhere and rested in no one place. They were the eyes which looked up to her now from Joan's face, and she felt suddenly divorced from her baby, as if all the blood in Joan were the blood of her father.

"He left you here alone?" she murmured.

The child looked at her with a sort of curious amazement.

"Joan isn't alone."

She whistled softly, and around the corner of the rock peered two tiny, beady-bright eyes, and the sharp nose of a coyote puppy. It disappeared at once at the sight of the stranger, and now all the strength went from Kate. She slipped helplessly down, and sat on a boulder trying to think, trying to master the panic which chilled her; for she thought of the day when Whistling Dan brought home to the Cumberland Ranch the wounded wolf-dog, Black Bart. But the call of Joan had traveled far, and now a squirrel came in at a gallop with his vast tail bobbing behind him, and ran right up the rock until he was on the shoulder of the child. From this point of vantage, however, he saw Kate, and was instantly on the floor of the cave and scurrying for the entrance, chattering with rage.

The wild things came to Joan as they came to her father, and the eyes of the child were the eyes of Dan Barry. It came home to Kate and she saw the truth for the first time in her life. She had struggled to win him away from his former life, but now she knew that it was not habit which controlled him, for he was wild by instinct, by nature. Just the tang of his untamed blood had turned the child to this; and a few days more of life with him would leave her wild forever.

"He left you alone here!" she repeated fiercely. "Where a thousand things might happen. Thank God I've found you."

Even if her words conveyed little meaning to Joan, the intonation carried a message which was perfectly clear.

"Don't you like Daddy Dan?"

"Joan, Joan, I love him! Of course."

140

But Joan sat with a dubious eye which quickly darkened into fear.

"Oh, Munner, don't take us back!"

Such horror and terror and sadness mixed! The tears rushed into the eyes of Kate.

'Do you want to stay here, sweetheart?"

"Yes, munner."

"Without me?"

At first Joan shook her head decidedly, but thereafter she quickly became thoughtful.

"No, except when we eat."

"You don't want me here at dinner-time? Poor munner will get so hungry."

A great concession was about to burst from the remorseful lips of Joan, but again second thought sobered her. She remained in a quandary, unable to speak.

"Don't you want me even when you wake up at night?"

"Why?"

"Because you're so afraid of the dark."

"Joan's not afraid. Oh, no! Joan loves the dark."

If Kate maintained a smile, it was a frozen grimace. It had only been a few days—hardly yesterday—that Joan left, and already she was a little stranger. Suppose Dan should refuse to come back himself; refuse even to give up Joan! She started up, clutching the hand of the child.

"Quick, Joan, we must go!"

"Joan doesn't want to go!"

"We'll go—for a little walk. We—we'll surprise Daddy Dan."

"But Daddy Dan won't come back for long, long time. Not till the sun is away down behind that hill."

That should mean two hours, at least, thought Kate. She could wait a little.

"Joan, what taught you not to be afraid of the dark?"

This problem made Joan look about for an answer, but at length she called softly: "Jackie!"

She waited, and then whistled; at once the bright eyes of the little coyote appeared around the edge of the rock.

"Come here!" she commanded.

He slunk out with his head turned towards Kate and

cowered at the feet of the child. And the mother cringed inwardly at the sight; all wild things which hated man instinctively with tooth and claw were the friends, the allies of Whistling Dan, and now Joan was stepping in her father's path. A little while longer and the last vestige of gentleness would pass from her. She would be like Dan Barry, following calls which no other human could even hear. It meant one thing: at whatever cost, Joan must be taken from Dan and kept away.

"Jackie sleeps near me," Joan was saying. "We can see in the dark, can't we, Jackie?"

She lifted her head, and the moment her compelling eyes left him, Jackie scooted for shelter. The first strangeness had worn away from Joan and she began to chatter away about life in the cave and how Satan played there by the firelight with Black Bart, and how, sometimes—wonderful sight!—Daddy Dan played with them. The recital was quite endless, as they pushed farther and farther into the shadows, and it was the uneasiness which the dim light raised in her that made Kate determine that the time had come to go home.

"Now," she said, "we're going for that walk."

"Not away down there!" cried Joan.

Kate winced.

"It's lots nicer here, munner. You'd ought to just see what we have to eat! And my, Daddy Dan knows how to fix things."

"Of course he does. Now put on your hat and your cloak, Joan."

"This is lots warmer, munner."

"Don't you like it?" she added in alarm, stroking the delicate fur.

"Take it off!"

Kate ripped away the fastenings and tossed the skin far away.

"Oh!" breathed Joan.

"It isn't clean! It isn't clean," cried Kate. "Oh, my poor, darling baby! Get your bonnet and your cloak, Joan, quickly."

"We're coming back?"

"Of course."

Joan trudged obediently to the side of the cave and produced both articles, sadly rumpled, and Kate buttoned her into them with trembling fingers. Something akin to cold made her shake now. It was very much like a child's fear of the dark.

But as she turned towards the entrance to the cave and caught the hand of Joan, the child wrenched herself free.

"We'll never come back," she wailed. "Munner, I won't go!"

"Joan, come to me this instant."

Grief and fear and defiance had set the child trembling, but what the mother saw was the glint of the eyes, uneasy, hunting escape with animal cunning. It turned her heart cold, and she knew, with a sad, full knowledge that Dan was lost forever and that only one power could save Joan. That power was herself.

"I won't go!"

"Joan!"

A resolute silence answered her, and when she went threateningly forward, Joan shrank into the shadows near the rock. It was the play of light striking slant-wise from the entrance, no doubt, but it seemed to Kate that a flicker of yellow light danced across the eyes of the child. And it stopped Kate—took her breath with a new terror. Dan Barry, in the old days, had lived a life as quiet as a summer's day until the time Jim Silent struck him down in the saloon; and she remembered how Black Bart had come for her and led her to the saloon, and how she found Dan lying on the floor, streaked with blood, very pale; and how she had kneeled by him in a panic, and how his eyes had opened and stared at her without answer and the yellow, inhuman light swirled in them until she rose and backed out the door and fled in a hysteria of fear up the road. That had been the beginning of the end for Dan Barry, that instant when his eyes changed; and now Joan —she ran at her swiftly and gathered her into her arms. One instant of wild struggling, and then the child lay still, her head straightened a little, a shrill whistle pealed through the cave.

143

Kate stopped that piercing call with her hand, but when she turned, she saw in the entrance the dark body of Bart and his narrow, snake-like head.

CHAPTER XXV

The Battle

"It's Dan," whispered Kate. "He's come."

"Maybe Daddy Dan sent Bart back alone, munner."

"Does he do that often? Come quickly, Joan. Run!"

She ran towards the entrance, stumbling over the uneven ground and dragging Joan behind her, but when they came close the wolf-dog bristled and sent down the cavern a low growl that stopped them like an invisible barrier. The softest sounds in his register were ominous warnings to those who did not know Black Bart, but Kate and Joan understood that this muttering, harsh thunder was an ultimatum. If she had worn her revolver, a light, beautifully mounted thirty-two which Dan had given her, Kate would have shot the wolf and gone on across his body; for she had learned from Whistling Dan to shoot quickly as one points a finger and straight by instinct. Even as she stood there bare-handed she looked about her desperately for a weapon, seeing the daylight and the promise of escape beyond and only this dumb beast between her and freedom.

Once before, many a year before, she had gone like this, with empty hands, and subdued Black Bart simply through the power of quiet courage and the human eye. She determined to try again.

"Stand there quietly, Joan. Don't move until I tell you."

She made a firm step towards Bart.

"Munner, he'll bite!"

"Hush, Joan. Don't speak!"

At her forward movement the wolf-dog flattened his belly to the rock, and she saw his forepaws, large, almost, as the hands of a man, dig and work for a purchase from which he could throw himself at her throat.

"Steady, Bart!"

His silence was more terrible than a snarl; yet she stretched out her hand and made another step. It brought a sharp tensing of the body of Bart—the fur stood up about his throat like the mane of a lion, and his eyes were a devilish green. Another instant she kept her place, and then she remembered the story of Haines,—how Bart had gone with his master to that killing at Alder. If he had killed once, he would kill again; wild as he had been on that other time when she quelled him, he had never before been like this. The courage melted out of her; she forgot the pleasant day outside; she saw only those blazing eyes and shrank back towards the center of the cave. The muscles of the wolf relaxed visibly, and not till that moment did she realize how close she had been to the crisis.

"Bad Bart!" cried Joan, running in between. "Bad, bad dog!"

"Stop, Joan! Don't go near him!"

But Joan was already almost to Bart. When Kate would have run to snatch the child away that deep, rattling growl stopped her again, and now she saw that Joan ran not the slightest danger. She stood beside the huge beast with her tiny fist raised.

"'I'll tell Daddy Dan on you," she shrilled.

Black Bart made a furtive, cringing movement towards the child, but instantly stiffened again and sent his warning down the cave to Kate. Then a shadow fell across the entrance and Dan stood there with Satan walking behind. His glance ran from the bristling body of Bart to Kate, shrinking among the shadows, and lingered without a spark of recognition.

"Satan," he ordered, "go on in to your place."

The black stallion glided past the master and came on until he saw Kate. He stopped, snorting, and then circled her with his head suspiciously high, and ears back until he reached the place where his saddle was usually hung.

There he waited, and Kate felt the eyes of the horse, the wolf, the man, and even Joan, curiously upon her.

"Evenin'," nodded Dan, "might you have come up for supper?"

That was all. Not a step towards her, not a smile, not a greeting, and between them stood Joan her hands clasped idly before her while she looked from face to face, trying to understand. All the pangs of heart which come to woman between girlhood and old age went burningly through Kate in that breathing space, and afterwards she was cold, and saw herself and all the others clearly.

"I haven't come for supper. I've come to bring you back, Dan."

Not that she had the slightest hope that he would come, but she watched him curiously, almost as if he were a stranger, to see how he would answer.

"Come back?" he echoed. "To the cabin?"

"Where else?"

"It ain't happy there." He started. "You come up here with us, Kate."

"And raise Joan like a young animal in a cave?"

He looked at her with wonder, and then at the child. "Ain't you happy, Joan, up here?"

"Oh, Daddy Dan, Joan's *so* happy!"

"You see," he said to Kate, "she's terribly happy."

It was his utter simplicity which convinced her that arguments and pleas would be perfectly useless. Just behind the cool command which she kept over herself now was hysteria. She knew that if she relaxed her purposefulness for an instant the love for him would rush over her, weaken her. She kept her mind clear and steady with a great effort which was like divorcing herself from herself. When she spoke, there was another being which stood aside listening in wonder to the words.

"You've chosen this life, Dan, I won't blame you for leaving me this time any more than I blamed you the other times. I suppose it isn't you. It's the same impulse, after all, that took you south after—after the wild geese." She stopped almost broken down by the memory, and then recalled herself sternly. "It's the same thing that led you away after MacStrann through the storm. But whether it's a weakness in you, or the force of something outside

147

your control, I see this thing clearly; we can't go on. This is the 'end."

He seemed troubled, vaguely, as a dog is anxious when it sees a child weep and cannot make out the reason.

"Oh, Dan," she burst out, "I love you more than ever! If it were I alone, I'd follow you to the end of the world, and live as you live, and do as you do. But it's Joan. She has to be raised as a child should be raised. She isn't going to live with—with wild horses and wolves all her life. And if she stays on here, don't you see that the same thing which is a curse in you will grow strong and be a curse in her? Don't you see it growing? It's in her eyes! Her step is too light. She's lost her fear of the dark. She's drifting back into wildness. Dan, she has to go with me back to the cabin!"

At that she saw him start again, and his hand went out with a swift, subtle gesture towards Joan.

"Let me have her! I have to have her! She's mine!" Then more gently: "You can come to see her whenever you will. And, finally pray God you will come and stay with us always."

He had stepped to Joan while she spoke, and his hands made a quick movement of cherishing about her golden head, without touching it. For the first and the last time in her life, she saw something akin to fear in his eyes.

"Kate, I can't come back. I got things to do—out here!"

"Then let me take her."

She watched the wavering in him.

"Things would be kind of empty if she was gone, Kate."

"Why?" she asked bitterly. "You say you have your work to do—out here?"

He considered this gravely.

"I dunno. Except that I sort of need her."

She knew from of old that such questions only puzzled him, and soon he would cast away the attempt to decide, and act. Action was his sphere. There was only one matter in which he was unfailingly, relentlessly the same, and that was justice. To that sense in him she would make her last appeal.

"Dan, I can't take her. I only ask you to see that I'm right. She belongs to me. I bought her with pain.

It was a staggering blow to Whistling Dan. He took off his sombrero and passed his hand slowly across his forehead, then looked at her with a dumb appeal.

"I only want you to do the thing you think is square, Dan."

Once more he winced.

Then, slowly: "I'm tryin' to be square. Tryin' hard. I know you got a claim in her. But it seems like I have, too. She's like a part of me, mostly. When she's happy, I feel like smilin' sort of. When she cries it hurts me so's I can't hardly stand it."

He paused, looking wistfully from the staring child to Kate.

He said with sudden illumination: "Let her do the judgin'! You ask her to go to you, and I'll ask her to come to me. Ain't that square?"

For a moment Kate hesitated, but as she looked at Joan it seemed to her that when she stretched out her arms to her baby nothing in the world could keep them apart.

"It's fair," she answered. Dan dropped to one knee.

"Joan, you got to make up your mind. If you want to stay with, with Satan—speak up, Satan!"

The stallion whinnied softly, and Joan smiled.

"With Satan and Black Bart"—the wolf-dog had glided near, and now stood watching—"and with Daddy Dan, you just come to me. But if you want to go to—to Munner, you just go." On his face the struggle showed—the struggle to be perfectly just. "If you stay here, maybe it'll be cold, sometimes when the wind blows, and maybe it'll be hard other ways. And if you go to munner, she always be takin' care of you, and no harm'll ever come to you and you'll sleep soft between sheets, and if you wake up in the night she'll be there to talk to you. And you'll have pretty little dresses with all kinds of colors on 'em, most like. Joan, do you want to go to munner, or stay here with me?"

Perhaps the speech was rather long for Joan to follow, but the conclusion was plain enough; and there was Kate, she also upon one knee and her arms stretched out.

149

"Joan, my baby, my darling!"

"Munner!" whispered the child and ran towards her.

A growl came up in the throat of Black Bart and then sank away into a whine; Joan stopped short, and turned her head.

"Joan!" cried Kate.

Anguish made her voice loud, and from the loudness Joan shrank, for there was never a harsh sound in the cave except the growl of Bart warning away danger. She turned quite around and there stood Daddy Dan, perfectly erect, quite indifferent, to all seeming, as to her choice. She went to him with a rush and caught at his hands.

"Oh, Daddy Dan, I don't want to go. Don't you want Joan?"

He laid a hand upon her head, and she felt the tremor of his fingers; the wolf-dog lay down at her feet and looked up in her face; Satan, from the shadows beyond, whinnied again.

After that there was not a word spoken, for Kate looked at the picture of the three, saw the pity in the eyes of Whistling Dan, saw the wonder in the eyes of Joan, saw the truth of all she had lost. She turned towards the entrance and went out, her head bowed, stumbling over the pebbles.

CHAPTER XXVI

The Test

The most that could be said of Rickett was that it had a courthouse and plenty of quiet so perfect that the minds of the office holders could turn and turn and hear no sound saving their own turning. There were, of course, more buildings than the courthouse, but not so many that they could not be grouped conveniently along one street. The hush which rested over Rickett was never broken except in the periods immediately after the spring and fall round-ups when the saloons and gaming tables were suddenly flooded with business. Otherwise it was a rare event indeed which injected excitement into the village.

Such an event was the gathering of Sheriff Pete Glass' posse.

There had been other occasions when Pete and officers before his time had combed the county to get the cream of the fighting men, but the gathering of the new posse became different in many ways. In the first place the call for members was not confined to the county, for though it stretched as large as many a minor European kingdom, it had not the population of a respectable manufacturing town, and Pete Glass went far beyond its bounds to get his trailers. Everywhere he had the posters set up and on the posters appeared the bait. The state began the game with a reward of three thousand dollars: the county plastered two thousand dollars on top of that to make it an even five: then the town of Alder dug into its deep pockets and produced twenty-five hundred, while disinterested parties added contributions which swelled the total to a round ten thousand. Ten thousand dollars reward for the man described below, dead or alive. Ten thousand dollars which might be earned by the investment of a single bullet and the pressure on trigger; and above this the fame which such a deed would bring—no wonder that the mountain-desert hummed through all its peaks and plains, and stirred to life. Moreover, the news had gone abroad, the tale of the Killing of Alder and everything that went before. It went West; it appeared in newspapers; it cropped up at firesides; it gave a spark of terror to a myriad conversations; and everyone in Rickett felt that the eye of the nation was upon it; every one in Rickett dreamed nightly of the man described: "Daniel Barry, called Whistling Dan, about five feet nine or ten, slender, black hair, brown eyes, age about thirty years."

Secretly, Rickett felt perfectly convinced that Sheriff Pete Glass alone could handle this fellow and trim his claws for they knew how many a "bad man" had built a reputation high as Babel and baffled posses and murdered right and left, until the little dusty man on the little dusty roan went out alone and came back alone, and another fierce name went from history into legend. However, there were doubters, since this affair had new earmarks. It had been buzzed abroad that Whistling Dan was not only the hunted, but also the hunter, and that he had pledged himself to strike down all the seven who first took his trail. Five of these were already gone; two remained, and of these two one was Vic Gregg, no despicable fighter himself, and the other was no less than the invincible little sheriff himself. To imagine the sheriff beaten in the speed of his draw or the accuracy of his shot was to imagine the First Cause, Infinity, or whatever else is inconceivable; nevertheless, there were such possibilities as bullets fired at night through the window, and attacks from the rear. So Rickett waited, and held its breath and kept its eyes rather more behind than in front.

In the meantime, there was no lack of amusement, for from the four corners, blown by the four winds, men rode out of the mountain-desert and drifted into Rickett to seek for a place on that posse. Twenty men, that was the goal the sheriff had set. Twenty men trained to a hair. Beside the courthouse was a shooting gallery not over-

152

much used except during the two annual seasons of prosperity and reckless spending, and Pete Glass secured this place to test out applicants. After they passed this trial they were mustered into his presence, and he gave them an examination for himself. Just what he asked them or what he told them could never be known, but some men came from his presence very red, and others extremely pale, and some men blustered, and some men swore, and some men rode hastily out of town and spoke not a word, but few, very few, were those who came out wearing a little badge on their vest with the pride of a Knight of the Garter. At first the hordes rode in, young and old, youths keen for a taste of adventure, rusty fellows who had once been noted warriors; but these early levies soon discovered that courage and willingness was not so much valued as accuracy, and the old-timers learned, also, that accuracy must be accompanied by speed; and even when a man possessed both these qualities of hand and eye the gentle, inscrutable little man in his office might still reject them for reasons they could not guess.

This one thing was certain: the next time Pete Glass ran for office he would be beaten even by a greaser. He made enemies at the rate of a hundred a day during that period of selection.

Still the twenty were not recruited to the full. Thirteen, fourteen, fifteen were gathered into the fold, but still five men were lacking to complete the toll. Most men would have started their man-hunt with that formidable force, but Pete Glass was methodical. In his own heart of hearts he would have given his hope of heaven to meet Barry face to face and hand to hand, and see which was the better man, but Pete Glass owed a duty to his state before he owed a duty to himself. He stuck to his first plan. And every day the inhabitants of Rickett gathered at the shooting gallery to watch the tests and wonder at the successes and smile at the failures.

It was a very hard test which the sheriff had imposed. A man stood to one side of the iron-plate back wall which served as the target. He stood entirely out of sight and through an aperture in the side wall, at a signal, he tossed a round ball of clay, painted white. The marksman stood a good ten paces off, and he must strike that clay ball as it passed across the target. The balls were so small that even to strike them when they were stationary was a difficult task, and to hit them in motion was enough to task, the quickest eye and the cunningest hand.

It was old Pop Giersberg who stood with his ancient forty-five behind the counter, with his feet braced, on this bright morning, and behind him half of Rickett was gathered.

"D'you give me warnin', son?" he inquired of the man at the counter.

"Nary a warnin'," grinned the other, who was one of the chosen fifteen.

He wished Pop well. So did they all, but they had seen every man fail for two days at that target and one and all they had their doubts. Pop had been a formidable man in his day, but now his hand was stiff and his hair was gray. He was at least twenty years older than he felt.

He had hardly finished asking his question when a white ball was tossed across the target. Up came the gun of Pop Giersberg, exploded, and the bullet clanged on the iron; the white ball floated idly on across the wall and disappeared on the other side.

"Gimme another chance!" pleaded Pop, with a quaver in his voice. "That was just a try to get my eye in shape."

"Sure," chuckled the deputy. "Everybody gets three tries. It ain't hardly nacheral to hit that ball the first crack. Leastways, nobody ain't done it yet. You jest keep your eye peeled, Pop, that ball will come out ag'in."

And Pop literally kept his eye peeled.

He had double reason to pray for success, for his "old woman" had smiled and shook her head when he allowed that he would try out for a place on that posse. All his nerves grew taut and keen. He waited.

Once more the white streak appeared and surely he who threw the ball had every wish to see Pop succeed, for he tossed it high and easily. Again the gun barked from Giersberg's hand, and again the ball dropped almost slowly out of sight.

"It's a trick!" gasped Pop. "It's something damned queer."

154

"They's a considerable pile of gents that think the same way you do," admitted the deputy sheriff, dryly.

Pop glared at him and gritted his teeth.

"Lead the damn thing on agin," he said, and muttered the rest of his sentence to himself. He jerked his hat lower over his eyes, spread his feet a little more, and got ready for the last desperate chance.

But fate was against Pop. Twenty years before he might have struck that mark if he had been in top condition, but to-day, though he put his very soul into the effort, and though the ball for the third time was lobbed with the utmost gentleness through the air, his bullet banged vainly against the sheet of iron and the white, inoffensive ball continued on its way.

Words came in the throat of Pop, reached his opened mouth, and died there. He thrust the gun back into its holster, and turned slowly toward the crowd. There was no smile to meet his challenging eye, for Pop was a known man, and though he might have failed to strike this elusive mark that was no sign that he would fail to hit something six feet in height by a couple in breadth. When he found that no mockery awaited him, a sheepish smile began at his eyes and wandered dimly to his lips.

"Well, gents," he muttered, "I guess I ain't as young as I was once. S'long!"

He shouldered his way to the door and was gone.

"That's about all, friends," said the deputy crisply. "I guess there ain't any more clamorin's for a place to-day?"

He swept the crowd with a complacent eye.

"If you got no objection," murmured a newcomer, who had just slipped into the room, "I'd sort of like to take a shot at that."

CHAPTER XXVII

The Sixth Man

It caused a quick turning of heads.

"I don't want to put you out none," said the applicant gently. His voice was extremely gentle, and there was about him all the shrinking aloofness of the naturally timid. The deputy looked him over with quiet amusement— slender fellow with the gentlest brown eyes—and then with a quick side glance invited the crowd to get in on the joke.

"You ain't puttin' me out," he assured the other. "Not if you pay for your own ammunition."

"Oh, yes," answered the would-be man-hunter, "I reckon I could afford that."

He was so serious about it that the crowd murmured its amusement instead of bursting into loud laughter. If the man was a fool, at least he was not aggressive in his folly. They gave way and he walked slowly towards the counter and stepped into the little open space beside the master of ceremonies. Very obviously he was ill at ease to find himself the center of so much attention.

"I s'pose you been practicin' up on tin-cans?" suggested the deputy, leaning on the counter.

"Sometimes I hit things and sometimes I don't," answered the stranger.

"Well," and this was put more crisply as the deputy brought out a large pad of paper, "jest gimme your name, partner."

"Joe Cumber." He grew still more ill at ease. "I hear that even if you hit the mark you got to talk to the sheriff himself afterwards?"

"Yep."

The applicant sighed.

"Why d'you ask?"

"I ain't much on words."

"But hell with your gun, eh?" The deputy sheriff grinned again, but when the other turned his head toward him, his smile went out, suddenly while the wrinkle of mirth still lay in his cheek. The deputy stroked his chin and looked thoughtful.

"Get your gun ready," he ordered.

The other slipped his hand down to his gun-butt and moved his weapon to make sure that it was perfectly loose in the leather.

"Ain't you goin' to take your gun out?" queried the deputy.

"Can I do that?"

"I reckon not," said the deputy, and looked the stranger straight in the eyes.

His change to deadly earnestness put a hush over the crowd.

Across the target, not tossed easily as it had been for Pop Giersberg, but literally thrown, darted the line of white, while the gun flipped out of its holster as if it possessed life of its own and spoke. The white line ended half way to the farther side of the target, and the revolver slid again into hiding.

A clamor of amazement broke from the crowd, but the deputy looked steadily, without enthusiasm, at the stranger.

"Joe Cumber," he said, when the noise fell away a little, "I guess you'll see the sheriff. Harry, take Joe Cumber up to Pete, will you?"

One of the bystanders jumped at the suggestion and led the other from the room, with a full half of the crowd following. The deputy remained behind, thoughtful.

"What's the matter?" asked one of the spectators. "You look like you'd seen a ghost."

"Gents," answered the deputy, "do any of you recollect seein' this feller before?"

They did not.

"They's something queer about him," muttered the deputy.

"He may be word-shy," proffered a wit, "but he sure ain't gun-shy!"

"When he looked at me," said the deputy, more to himself than to the others, "it seemed to me like they was a swirl of yaller come into his eyes. Made me feel like some one had sneaked up behind me with a knife."

In his thoughtfulness his eyes wandered, and wandering, they fell upon the notice of the reward for the capture, dead or alive, of Daniel Barry, about five feet nine or ten, slender, with black hair and brown eyes.

"My God!" cried the deputy.

But then he relaxed against the counter.

"It ain't possible," he murmured.

"What ain't possible?"

"However, I'm goin' to go and hang around. Gents, I got a crazy idea."

He had no sooner started toward the door than he seemed to gain surety out of the motion.

"It's him!" he cried. He turned toward the others, white of face. "Come on, all of you! It's him! Barry!"

But in the meantime "Harry" had gone on swiftly to the office of the sheriff with "Joe Cumber." Behind him swirled the curious crowd and for their benefit he asked his questions loudly.

"Partner, that was sure a pretty play you made. I've seen 'em all try out to crack them balls, but I never seen none do it the way you did—with your gun in the leather at the start. What part of the country might you be from?"

The other answered gently: "Why, from over yonder."

"The T O outfit, eh?"

"Beyond that."

"Up in the Gray Mountains? That so! I s'pose you been on trails like this before?"

"Nothin' to talk about."

There might have been a double meaning in this remark, and Harry looked twice to make sure that there was no guile.

"Well, here we are." He threw open a door which revealed a bald-headed clerk seated at a desk in a little bare room. "Billy, here's a gent that cracked it the first whack and started his gun from the leather, by God. He——"

158

"Jest kindly close the door, Harry," said Billy. "Step in, partner. Gimme your name?"

The door closed on the discomfited Harry, and "Joe Cumber" stood close to it, apparently driven to shrinking into the wall in his embarrassment, but while he stood there his hand fumbled behind him and turned the key in the lock, and then extracted it.

"My name's Joe Cumber."

"Joe Cumber,"—this while inscribing it.

"Age?"

"About thirty-two, maybe."

"Don't you know?"

"I don't exactly."

His eyes were as vague as his words, gentle, and smiling.

"Thirty-two?" said Billy sharply. "You look more like twenty-five to me. S'pose we split the difference, eh?"

And with a grin he wrote: "Age twenty-two or three."

"Business?"

"Trapper."

"Good! The sheriff is pretty keen for 'em. You gents in that game got a sort of nose for the trail, mostly. All right, Cumber, you'll see Glass."

He stood at the door.

"By the way, Cumber, is that straight about startin' your shot with your gun in the holster?"

"I s'pose it is."

"You s'pose?" grunted the Clerk. "Well, come on in."

He banged once on the door and threw it open.

"Joe Cumber, Pete. And he drilled the ball startin' his gun out of the leather. Here's his card."

He closed the door, and once more the stranger stood almost cringing against it, and once more his fingers deftly turned the key—softly, silently—and extracted it from the lock.

The sheriff had not looked up from the study of the card, for reading was more difficult to him than man-killing, and Joe Cumber had an opportunity to examine the room. It was hung with a score of pictures. Some large, some small, but most of them enlargements, it was apparent of kodak snapshots, for the eyes had that bleary

159

look which comes in photographs spread over ten times their intended space. The faces had little more than bleary eyes in common, for there were bearded men, and smooth-shaven faces, and lean and fat men; there were round, cherubic countenances, and lean, hungry heads; there were squared, protruding chins, and there were chins which sloped away awkwardly toward the neck; in fact it seemed that the sheriff had collected twenty specimens to represent every phase of weakness and strength in the human physiognomy. But beneath the pictures, almost without exception, there hung weapons: rifles, revolvers, knives, placed criss-cross in a decorative manner, and it came to "Joe Cumber" that he was looking at the galaxy of the dead who had fallen by the hand of Sheriff Pete Glass. Not a face meant anything to him but he knew, instinctively, that they were the chosen bad men of the past twenty years.

"So you're Joe Cumber?"

The sheriff turned in his swivel chair and tossed his cigarette butt through the open window.

"What can I do for you?"

"I got an idea, sheriff, that maybe you'd sort of like to have my picture."

The sheriff looked up from his study of the card, and having looked up his eyes remained riveted. The other no longer cringed with embarrassment, but every line of his body breathed a great happiness. He was like one who has been riding joyously, with a sharp wind in his face.

There was a distant rushing of feet, a pounding on the door of the next room.

"What's that?" muttered the sheriff, his attention called away.

"They want me."

"Wait a minute," called the voice of Billy without.

"I'll open the door. By God, it's locked!"

"They want me—five feet nine, or ten, slender, black hair and brown eyes——"

"Barry!"

"Glass, I've come for you."

"And I'm ready. And I'll say this"—he was standing, now, and his nervous hands were at his sides—"I been

160

hungerin' and hopin' for this time to come. Barry, before you die, I want to thank you!"

"You've followed me like a skunk," said Barry, "from the time you killed a hoss that had never done no harm to you. You got on my trail when I was livin' peacable."

There was a tremendous beating on the outer door of the other room, but Barry went on: "You took a gent that was livin' straight and you made a sneak and a crook out of him and sent him to double-cross me. You ain't worth livin'. You've spent your life huntin' men, and now you're at the end of your trail. Think it over. You're ready to kill agin, but are you ready to die?"

The little dusty man grew dustier still. His mouth worked.

"Damn you," he whispered, and went for his gun.

It was out, his finger on the trigger, the barrel whipping into line, when the weapon in Barry's hand exploded. The sheriff spun on his heel and fell on his face. Three times, as he lay there, dead in all except the instinctive movement of his muscles, his right hand clawed at the empty holster at his side. The sixth man had died for Grey Molly.

The outer door of Billy's room crashed to the floor, and heavy feet thundered nearer. Barry ran to the window and whistled once, very high and thin. It brought a black horse racing around a corner nearby; it brought a wolf-dog from an opposite direction, and as they drew up beneath the window, he slid out and dropped lightly, cat-like, to the ground. One leap brought him to the saddle, and Satan stretched out along the street.

161

CHAPTER XXVIII

The Blood of the Father

On the night of her failure at the cave, Kate came back to the cabin and went to her room without any word to Buck or Lee Haines, but when they sat before the fire, silent, or only murmuring, they could hear her moving about. Whatever sleep they got before morning was not free from dreams, for they knew that something was impending, and after breakfast they learned what it was. She struck straight out from the shoulder. She was going up to the cave and if Dan was away she would take Joan by force; she needed help: would they give it? They sat for a long time, looking at each other and then avoiding Kate with their eyes. It was not the fear of death but of something more which both of them connected with the figure of Whistling Dan. It was not until she took her light cartridge belt from the wall and buckled on her gun that they rose to follow. Before the first freshness of the morning passed they were winding up the side of the mountain, Kate a little in the lead, for she alone knew the way.

Where they rounded the shoulder, the men reined the horses with which Kate had provided them and sat looking solemnly at each other.

"Maybe we'll have no chance to talk alone again," said Lee Haines. "This is the last trail either for Barry or for us. And I don't think that Barry is that close to the end of his rope. Buck, give me your hand and say goodby. All that a man can do against Whistling Dan, and that isn't much, I'll do. Having you along won't make us a whit stronger."

"Thanks," growled Buck Daniels. "Jes save that kind

farewell till I show yaller. Hurry up, she's gettin' too far ahead."

At the bottom of the ravine, where they dismounted for the precipitous slope above, Kate showed her first hesitation.

"You both know what it means?" she asked them.

"We sure do," replied Buck.

"Dan will find out that you've helped me, and then he'll never forgive you. Will you risk even that?"

"Kate," broke in Lee Haines, "don't stop for questions. Keep on and we'll follow. I don't *want* to think of what may happen."

She turned without a word and went up the steep incline.

"What d'you think of your soft girl now?" panted Buck at the ear of Haines. The latter flashed a significant look at him but said nothing. They reached the top of the canyon wall and passed on among the boulders.

Kate had drawn back to them now, and they walked as cautiously as if there were dried leaves under foot. She had only lifted a finger of warning, and they knew that they were near to the crisis. She came to the great rock around which she had first seen the entrance to the cave on the day before. Inch by inch, with Buck and Lee following her example, they worked toward the edge of the boulder and peered carefully around it.

There opened the cave, and in front of it was Joan playing with what seemed to be a ball of gray fur. Her hair tumbled loose and bright about her shoulders; she wore the tawny hide which Kate had seen before, and on her feet, since the sharp rocks had long before worn out her boots, she had daintily fashioned moccasins. Bare knees, profusely scratched, bare arms rapidly browning to the color of the fur she wore, Haines and Buck had to rub their eyes and look again before they could recognize her.

They must have made a noise—perhaps merely an intaking of breath inaudible even to themselves but clear to the ears of Joan. She was on her feet, with bright, wild eyes glancing here and there. There was no suggestion of childishness in her, but a certain willingness to flee from a great danger or attack a weaker force. She stood alert, rather than frightened, with her head back as if she scented the wind to learn what approached. The ball of gray fur straightened into the sharp ears and the flashing teeth of a coyote puppy. Buck Daniels' foot slipped on a pebble and at the sound the coyote darted to the shadow of a little shrub and crouched there, hardly distinguishable from the shade which covered it, and the child with infinitely cunning instinct, raced to a patch of yellow sand and tawny rocks among which she cowered and remained there motionless.

One thing at least was certain. Whistling Dan was not in the cave, for if he had been the child would have run to him for protection, or at least cried out in her alarm. This information Haines whispered to Kate and she nodded, turning a white face toward him. Then she stepped out from the rock and went straight toward Joan.

There was no stir in the little figure. Even the wind seemed to take part in the secret and did not lift the golden hair. Once the eyes of the child glittered as they turned toward Kate, but otherwise she made no motion, like a rabbit which will not budge until the very shadow of the reaching hand falls over it.

So it was with Joan, and as Kate leaned silently over her she sprang to her feet and darted between the hands of her mother and away among the rocks. Past the reaching hands of Lee Haines she swerved, but it was only to run straight into the grip of Buck Daniels. Up to that moment she had not uttered a sound, but now she screamed out, twisted in his arms, and beat furiously against his face.

"Joan!". cried Kate. "Joan!"

She reached Buck and unwound his arms from the struggling body of the child.

"Honey, why are you afraid? Oh, my baby!"

For an instant Joan stood free, wavering, and her eyes held steadily upon her mother bright with nothing but fear and strangeness. Then something melted in her little round face, she sighed.

"Munner!" and stole a pace closer. A moment later Kate sat with Joan in her arms, rocking to and fro and weeping.

"What's happened?" gasped Haines to Daniels. "What's happened to the kid?"

"Don't talk," answered Buck, his face gray as that of Kate. "It's Dan's blood."

He drew a great breath.

"Did you see her try to—to bite me while I was holdin' her?"

Kate had started to her feet, holding Joan in one arm and dashing away her tears with the free hand. All weakness was gone from her.

"Hurry!" she commanded. "We haven't any time to lose. Buck, come here! No, Lee, you're stronger. Honey, this is your Uncle Lee. He'll take care of you; he won't hurt you. Will you go to him?"

Joan shrank away while she examined him, but the instincts of a child move with thrice the speed of a mature person's judgment: she read the kindly honesty which breathed from every line of Haines' face, and held out her arms to him.

Then they started down the slope for the horses, running wildly, for the moment they turned their backs on the cave the same thought was in the mind of each, the same haunting fear of that small, shrill whistle pursuing. Half running, half sliding, they went down to the bottom of the gorge. While the pebble they started rushed after them in small avalanches, and they even had to dodge rocks of considerable size which came bounding after, Joan, alert upon the shoulder of Lee Haines, enjoyed every moment of it; her hair tossed in the sun, her arms were outstretched for balance. So they reached the horses, and climbed into the saddles. Then, without a word from one to the other, but with many a backward look they started on the flight.

By the time they reached the shoulder of the hill on the farther side, with a long stretch of down slope before, they had placed a large handicap between them and the danger of pursuit, but still they were not at ease. On their trail, sooner or later, would come three powers working towards one end, the surety of Black Bart following a scent, the swiftness of Satan which never tired, and above all the rider who directed them both and kept them to their work.

His was the arm which could strike from the distance and bring them down. They spurted down the hill.

No sooner were they in full motion than Joan, for the first time, seemed to realize what it was all about. She was still carried by Lee Haines, who cradled her easily in his powerful left arm, but now she began to struggle. Then she stiffened and screamed: "Daddy Dan! Daddy Dan!"

"For God's sake, stop her mouth or he'll hear!" groaned Buck Daniels.

"He can't!" said Haines. "We're too far away even if he were at the cave now."

"I tell you he'll hear! Don't talk to me about distance." Kate reined her horse beside Lee.

"Joan!" she commanded.

They were sweeping across the meadow now at an easy gallop. Joan screamed again, a wild plea for help.

"Joan!" repeated Kate, and her voice was fierce. She raised her quirt and shook it. "Be quiet, Munner whip —hard!"

Another call died away on the lips of Joan. She looked at her mother with astonishment and then with a new respect.

"If you cry once more, munner whip!"

And Joan was silent, staring with wonder and defiance.

When they came close to the cabin, Lee Haines drew rein, but Kate motioned him on.

"Where to?" he called.

"Back to the old ranch," she answered. "We've got to have help."

He nodded in grim understanding, and they headed on and down the slope towards the valley.

CHAPTER XXIX

Billy the Clerk

If Sheriff Pete Glass had been the typical hard riding, sure-shooting officer of the law as it is seen in the mountain-desert, his work would have died with his death, but Glass had a mind as active as his hands, and therefore, for at least a little while, his work went on after him. He had gathered fifteen practiced fighters who represented, it might be said, the brute body of the law, and when they, with most of Rickett at their heels, burst down the door of the Sheriff's office and found his body, they had only one thought, which was to swing into the saddle and ride on the trail of the killer, who was even now in a diminishing cloud of dust down the street. He was riding almost due east, and the cry went up: "He's streakin' it for the Morgan Hills. Git after him, boys!" So into the saddle they went with a rush, fifteen tried men on fifteen chosen horses, and went down the street with a roar of hoof-beats. That was the body and muscle of the sheriff's work going out to avenge him, but the mind of the law remained behind.

It was old Billy, the clerk. No one paid particular attention to Billy, and they never had. He was useless on a horse and ridiculous with a gun, and the only place where he seemed formidable was behind a typewriter. Now he sat looking down into the dead face of Pete Glass, trying to grasp the meaning of it all. From the first he had been with Pete, from the first the invincibility of the little dusty man had been the chief article of Billy's creed, and now his dull eyes, bleared with thirty years of clerical labor, wandered around on the galaxy of dead men who looked down at him from the wall. He leaned over and took the hand of the sheriff as one would lean to help up a fallen man, but the fingers were already growing cold, and then Billy realized for the first time that this was death. Pete Glass had been; Pete Glass was not.

Next he knew that something had to be done, but what it was he could not tell, for he sat in the sheriff's office and in that room he was accustomed to stop thinking and receive orders. He went back to his own little cubby-hole, and sat down behind the typewriter; at once his mind cleared, thoughts came, and linked themselves into ideas, pictures, plans.

The murderer must be taken, dead or alive, and those fifteen men had ridden out to do the necessary thing. They had seemed irresistible, as they departed; indeed, no living thing they met could withstand them, human or otherwise, as Billy very well knew. Yet he recalled a saying of the sheriff, a thing he had insisted upon: "No man on no hoss will ever ride down Whistlin' Dan Barry. It's been tried before and it's never worked. I've looked up his history and it can't be done. If he's goin' to be run down it's got to be done with relays, like you was runnin' down a wild hoss. Billy rubbed his bald head and thought and thought.

With that orderliness which had become his habit of mind, from work with reports and papers, sorting and filing away, Billy went back to the beginning. Dan Barry was fleeing. He started from Rickett, and nine chances out of ten he was heading, eventually, towards those practically impenetrable mountain ranges where the sheriff before had lost the trail after the escape from the cabin and the killing of Mat Henshaw. Towards this same region, again, he had retreated after the notorious Killing at Alder. There was no doubt, then, humanly speaking, that he would make for the same safe refuge.

At first glance this seemed quite improbable, to be sure, for the Morgan Hills lay due east, or very nearly east, while the place from which Barry must have sallied forth and to which he would return was somewhere well north of west, and a good forty miles away. It seemed strange that he should strike off in the opposite direction, so Billy closed his eyes, leaned back in his chair, and summoned up a picture of the country.

Five miles to the east the Morgan Hills rolled, sharply broken ups and downs of country—bad lands rather than real hills, and a difficult region to keep game in view. That very idea gave Billy his clue. Barry knew that he would be followed hard and fast, and he headed straight for the Morgan's to throw the posse off the final direction he intended to take in his flight. In spite of the matchless speed of that black stallion of which the sheriff had learned so much, he would probably let the posse keep within easy view of him until he was deep within the bad-lands. Then he would double sharply around and strike out in the true direction of his flight.

Having reached this point in his deductions, Billy smote his hands together. He was trembling with excitement so that he filled his pipe with difficulty. By the time it was drawing well he was back examining his mental picture of the country.

West of Rickett about the same distance as Morgan Hills, ran the Wago Mountains, low, rolling ranges which would hardly form an impediment for a horseman. Across these Barry might cut at a good speed on his western course, but some fifteen or twenty miles from Rickett he was bound to reach a most difficult barrier. It was the Asper river, at this season of the year swollen high and swift with snow-water,— rare feat indeed if a man could swim his horse across such a stream. There were only two places in which it could be forded.

About fifty miles north and a little east of the line from Rickett the Asper spread out into a broad, shallow bed, its streams dispersed for several miles into a number of channels which united again, farther down the course, and made the same strong river. Towards this ford, therefore, it was possible that Dan Barry would head, in the region of Caswell City.

There was, however, another way of crossing the stream. Almost due west of Rickett, a distance of fifteen miles, Tucker Creek joined the Asper. Above the point of junction both the creek and the river were readily fordable, and Barry could cross them and head straight for his goal.

It was true that to make Tucker Creek he would have to double out of the Morgan Hills and brush back perilously close to Rickett, but Billy was convinced that this was the outlaw's plan; for though the Caswell City fords would be his safest route it would take him a day's ride, on an ordinary horse, out of his way. Besides, the sheriff had always said: "Barry will play the chance!"

Billy would have ventured his life that the fugitive would strike straight for the Creek as soon as he doubled out of Morgan Hills.

Doors began to bang; a hundred pairs of boots thudded and jingled towards Billy; the noise of voices rolled through the outer hall, poured through the door, burst upon his ears. He looked up in mild surprise; the first wave of Rickett's men had swept out of the courthouse to take the trail of the fugitive or to watch the pursuit; in this second wave came the remnants, the old men, the women; great-eyed children. In spite of their noise of foot and voice they appeared to be trying to walk stealthily, talk softly. They leaned about his desk and questioned him with gesticulations, but he only stared. They were all dim as dream people to Billy the clerk, whose mind was far away struggling with his problem.

"Pore old Billy is kind of dazed," suggested a woman. "Don't bother him, Bud. Look here!"

The tide of noise and faces broke on either side of the desk and swayed off towards the inner office and vaguely Billy felt that they should not be there—the sheriff's privacy—the thought almost drew him back to complete consciousness, but he was borne off from them, again, on a wave of study, pictures. Off there to the east went the fifteen best men of the mountain-desert on the trail of the slender fellow with the black hair and the soft brown eyes. How he had seemed to shrink with aloofness, timidity, when he stood there at the door, giving his name. It was not modesty. Billy knew now, it was something akin to the beasts of prey, who shrink from the eyes of men until they are mad with hunger, and in the slender man Billy remembered the same shrinking, the same hunger. When he struck, no wonder that even the Sheriff went down; no wonder if even the fifteen men were baffled on

170

that trail; and therefore, it was sufficiently insane for him, Billy the clerk, to sit in his office and dream with his ineffectual hands of stopping that resistless flight. Yet he pulled himself back to his problem.

Considering his problem in general, the thing was perfectly simple: Barry was sure to head west, and to the west there were only two gates—fording the creek and the river above the junction in the first place, or in the second place cutting across the Asper far north as Caswell City.

If he could be turned from the direction of Tucker Creek he would head for the second possible crossing, and when he drew near Caswell City if he were turned by force of numbers again he would unquestionably skirt the Asper, hoping against hope that he might find a fordable place as he galloped south. But, going south, he might be fenced again from Tucker Creek, and then his case would be hopeless and his horse worn down.

It was a very clever plan, quite simple after it was once conceived, but in order to execute it properly it was necessary that the outlaw be pressed hard every inch of the way and never once allowed to get out of sight. He must be chased with relays. In ordinary stretches of the mountain-desert that would have been impossible, but the country around Rickett was not ordinary.

Between the Morgan Hills and Wago there were considerable stretches of excellent farm land in the center of which little towns had grown up. Running north from the county seat, they were St. Vincent, Wago, and Caswell City. Coming south along the Asper River there were Ganton and Wilsonville, and just above the junction of the river with Tucker Creek lay the village of Bly Falls. There was no other spot in the mountain-desert, perhaps, which could show so many communities. Also it was possible to get in touch with the towns from Rickett, for in a wild spirit of enterprise telephones had been strung to connect each village of the group.

His hand went out mechanically and pushed in an open drawer of his filing cabinet as if he were closing up the affair, putting away the details of the plan. Each point was now clear, orderly, assembled. It meant simply chasing

Barry along a course which covered close to a hundred miles and which lay in a loosely shaped U. St. Vincent's was the tip of the eastern side of that U. The men of St. Vincent's were to be called out to turn the outlaw out of his course towards Tucker Creek, and then, as he struck northeast towards Caswell City, they were to furnish the posse with fifteen fresh horses, the best they could gather on such short notice. Swinging north along that side of the U, Wago would next be warned to get its contribution of fifteen horses ready, and this fresh relay would send Barry thundering along towards Caswell City at full speed. Then Caswell City would send out its contingent of men and horses, and turn the fugitive back from the fords. By this time unless his horse were better winded than any that Billy had ever dreamed of, it would be staggering at every stride, and the fresh horses from Caswell City would probably ride him down before he had gone five miles. Even in case they failed in this, there was the little town of Ganton, which would be ready with its men and mounts. Perhaps they could hem in the desperado from the front and shoot him down there, as he skirted along the river. At the worst they would furnish the fresh horses and the fifteen hardy riders would spur at full speed south along the river. If again, by some miracle, the black stallion lasted out this run, Wilsonville lay due ahead, and that place would again give new horses to the chase.

Last of all, the men of Bly Falls could be warned. Bly Falls was a town of size and it could turn out enough men to block a dozen Dan Barry's, no matter how desperate. If he reached that point, he must turn back. The following posse would catch him from the rear, and between two fires he must die ingloriously. Taking the plan as a whole it meant running Barry close to a hundred miles with six sets of horses.

It all hinged, however, on the first step: Could the men of St. Vincent turn him out of his western course and send him north towards Caswell City. If they could, he was no better than a dead man. All things favored Billy. In the first place it was still morning, and eight hours of broad daylight would keep the fugitive in view every inch of the way. In the second place, much of the distance was cut up by the barb-wire fences of the farm-lands, and he must either jump these or else stop to cut them.

A crackle of laughter cut in on Billy the clerk. They were laughing in that inner office, where the sheriff lay dead. Blood swept across his eyes, set his brain whirling, and he rushed to the door.

"You yelpin' coyotes!" shouted Billy the clerk. "Get out. I got to be alone! Get out, or by God———"

It was not so much his words, or the fear of his threats, but the very fact that Billy the clerk, harmless, smiling old Billy, had burst into noisy wrath, scared them as if an earthquake had gripped the building. They went out sidling, and left the rooms in quiet. Then Billy took up the phone.

"Pete Glass is dead," he was saying a moment later to the owner of the general merchandise store at St. Vincent. "Barry came in this morning and shot him. The boys have run him east to the Morgan Hills. Johnny, listen hard and shut up. You got half an hour to turn out every man in your town. Ride south till you get in the hills on a bee-line east of where Tucker Creek runs into the old Asper. D'you hear? Then keep your eyes peeled to the east, and watch for a man on a black hoss ridin' hard, because Barry is sure as hell goin' to double back out of the Morgan Hills and come west like a scairt coyote. The posse will be behind him, but they most like be a hell of a ways to the bad. Johnny, everything hangs on your turnin' Barry back. And have fifteen fresh hosses, the best St. Vincent has, so that the boys in the posse can climb on 'em and ride hell-bent for Wago. Johnny, if we get him started north he's dead—and if you turn him like I say I'll see that you come in on the reward. D'ye hear?"

But there was only an inarticulate whoop from the other end of the wire.

Billy hung up. A little later he was talking to Wago.

CHAPTER XXX

The Morgan Hills

Once out of Rickett, Barry pulled the stallion back to an easy canter. He had camped during the latter part of the night near the town and ridden in in the morning, so that Satan was full of running. He rebelled now against this easy pace, and tossed his head with impatience. No curb restrained him, not even a bit; the light hackamore could not have held him for an instant, but the voice of the rider kept him in hand. Now, out of Rickett's one street, came the thing for which Barry had waited, and delayed his course—a scudding dust cloud. On the top of a rise of ground he brought Satan to a halt and looked back, though Black Bart ran in a circle around him, and whined anxiously. Bart knew that they should be running; there was no good in that ragged dust-cloud. Finally he sat down on his haunches and looked his master in the face, quivering with eagerness. The posse came closer, at the rate of a racing horse, and near at hand the tufts of dust which tossed up above and behind the riders dissolved, and Whistling Dan made out clearly, and more clearly.

For one form he looked above all, a big man who rode somewhat slanting; but Vic Gregg was not among the crowd, and for the rest, Barry had no wish to come within range of their harm. The revolver at his side, the rifle in the case, were for the seventh man who must die for Grey Molly. These who followed him mattered nothing—except that he must not come within their reach. He studied them calmly as they swept nearer, fifteen chosen men as he could tell by their riding, on fifteen choice horses as he could tell by their gait. If they pushed him into a corner—

174

well, five men were odds indeed, yet he would not have given them a thought; ten men made it a grim affair, but still he might have taken a chance; however, fifteen men made a battle suicide—he simply must not let them corner him. Particularly fifteen such men as these, for in the mountain-desert where all men are raised gun in hand, these were the quickest and the surest marksmen. Each one of them had struck that elusive white ball in motion, and each had done it with a revolver. What could they do with a rifle?

That thought might have sent him rushing Satan down the farther slope, but instead, he raised his head a little more and began to whistle softly to himself. Satan locked an ear back to listen; Black Bart rose with a muffled growl. The posse rode in clear view now, and at their head was a tall, lean man with the sun glinting now and again on his yellow moustaches. He threw out his arm and the posse scattered towards the left. Obviously he was the accepted leader, and indeed few men in the mountain-desert would not willingly have followed Mark Retherton. Another gesture from Retherton, and at once a dozen guns gleaned, and a dozen bullets whizzed perilously close to Barry, then the reports came barking up to him; he was just a little out of range.

Still he lingered for a moment before he turned Satan reluctantly, it seemed and started him down the far slope, straightaway for the Morgan Hills as old Billy had prophesied. It would be no exercise canter even for Satan, for the horses which followed were rare of their kind, and the western horse at the worst has manifold fine points. His ancestor is the Barb or the Arab which the Spaniards brought with them to Mexico and the descendants of that finest of equine bloods made up the wild herds which soon roamed the mountain-desert to the north. Long famines of winter, hot deserts in summer, changed their appearance. Their heads grew lumpier, their necks more scraggy, their croups more slanting, their legs shorter; but their hoofs grew denser, hardier, their shorter coupling gave them great weight-carrying possibilities, the stout bones and the clean lines of their legs meant speed, and above all they kept the stout heart of the thoroughbred and they gained more than this, an indomitable, bulldog persistence. The cheapest Western cow-pony may look like the cartoon of a horse, but he has points which a judge will note, and he will run a picture horse to death in three days.

Such were the horses which took the trail of Satan and they were chosen specimens of their kind. Up the slope they stormed and there went Satan skimming across the hollow beneath them. Their blood was his blood, their courage his courage, their endurance his endurance. The difference between them was the difference between the factory machine and the hand made work of art. From his pasterns to his withers, from his hoofs to his croup every muscle was perfectly designed and perfectly placed for speed, tireless running; every bone was the maximum of lightness and strength combined. A feather bloom on a steady wind, such was the gait of Satan.

Down the hollow the posse thundered, and up the farther slope, and still the black slipped away from them until Mark Retherton cursed deeply to himself.

"Don't race your hosses, boys," he shouted. "Keep 'em in hand. That devil is playing with us."

As a result, they checked their mounts to merely a fast gallop, and Barry, looking back, laughed softly with understanding. Far different the laborious pounding of the posse and the light stretch of Satan beneath him. He leaned a little until he could catch the sound of the breathing, big, steady draughts with comfortable intervals between. He could run like that all day, it seemed, and Whistling Dan ran his fingers luxuriously down the shining neck. Instantly the head tossed up, and a short whinny whipped back to him like a question. Just before them the Morgan Hills jutted up, like stiff mud chopped by the tread of giants.

"Now, partner," murmured Barry, "show 'em what you can do! Jest lengthen out a bit."

The steady breeze from the running sharpened into a gale, whisking about his face; there was no longer the wave-like rock of that swinging gallop but a smooth, swift succession of impulses. Rocks, shrubs darted past him, and he felt a gradual settling of the horse beneath him as the strides lengthened. From behind a yell of dismay, and with a backward glance he saw every man of the posse leaning forward and swinging his quirt. An instant later half a dozen of the ragged little hills closed between them.

Once fairly into the heart of the Morgans, he called the stallion back from the racing stride to a long canter, and from the gallop to a rapid trot, for in this broken country it was wearing on an animal to maintain a lope up hill and down the quick, jerking falls. The cowpuncher hates the trot, for his ponies are not built for it, but the deep play of Satan's fetlock joints broke the hard impacts; his gait now was hardly more jarring than the flow of the single-foot in an ordinary animal.

Black Bart, who had been running directly under the nose of the stallion, now skirted away in the lead. Here and there he twisted among the gulleys at a racing clip, his head high, and always he picked out the smoothest ground, the easiest rise, the gentlest descent which lay more or less straight in the line of his master's flight. It cut down the work of the stallion by half to have this swift, sure scout run before and point out the path, yet it was stiff labor at the best and Barry was glad when he came on the hard gravel of an old creek bed cutting at right angles to his course.

From the first he had intended to run towards the Morgans only to cover the true direction of his flight, and now, since the posse was hopelessly left behind him, well out of hearing, he rode Satan into the middle of the creek bed and swung him north.

It was bad going for a horse carrying a rider, and even the catlike certainty of Satan's tread could not avoid sharp edges here and there that might cut his hoofs. So Barry leaped to the ground and ran at full speed down the bed. Behind him Satan followed, his ears pricked uneasily, and Black Bart, at a signal from his master, dropped back and remained at the first bend of the old, empty stream. In a moment they wound out of sight even of Bart, but Barry kept steadily on. It would take a magnifying glass to read his trail over those rocks.

He had covered a mile, perhaps, when Bart came scurrying again and leaped joyously around the master.

"They've hit the creek, eh?" said Whistling Dan. "Well, they'll mill around a while and like as not they'll run a course south to pick me up agin."

He gestured toward the side, and as soon as Satan stood on the good going once more, Barry swung into the saddle and headed straight back west. No doubt the posse would ride up and down the creek bed until they found his trail turning back, but they would lose precious minutes picking it up, and in the meantime he would be far, far away toward the ford of Tucker Creek. Then, clearly, but no louder than the snapping of a dry twig near his ear, he heard the report of a revolver and it spoke to him of many things as the baffled posse rode up and down the creek bed hunting for the direction of his escape. Some one had fired that shot to relieve his anger.

He neither spoke to Satan nor struck him, but there was a slight leaning forward, an imperceptible flexing of the leg muscles, and in response the black sprang again into the swift trot which sent him gliding over the ground, and twisting back and forth among the sharp-sided gullies with a movement as smooth as the run of the wolf-dog, which once again raced ahead.

When they came out in view of the rolling plain Barry stopped again and glanced to the west and the north, while Black Bart ran to the top of the nearest hill and looked back, an ever vigilant outpost. To the north lay the fordable streams near Caswell City, and that way was perfect safety, it seemed. Not perfect, perhaps, for Barry knew nothing of the telephones by which the little bald headed clerk at the sheriff's office was rousing the country-side, but if he struck toward Caswell City from the Morgans, there was not a chance in ten that scouts would catch him at the river which was fordable for mile after mile.

That way, then, lay the easiest escape, but it meant a long detour out of the shortest course, which struck almost exactly west, skirting dangerously close to Rickett. But, as Billy had presupposed, it was the very danger which lured the fugitive. Behind him, entangled in the gullies of the bad-lands, were the fifteen best men of the mountain-desert. In front of him lay nothing except the mind of Billy the clerk. But how could he know that?

Once more he swayed a little forward and this time the stallion swung at once into his ranging gallop, then verged into a half-racing gait, for Barry wished to get out of sight among the rolling ground before the posse came out from the Morgan Hills on his back trail.

CHAPTER XXXI

The Trap

He had already covered a good ten miles, and a large part of that through extremely rough going, but the black ran with his head as high as the moment he pulled out of Rickett that morning, and there was only enough sweat to make his slender neck and greyhound flanks flash in the sun. Back he winged toward Rickett, running as freely as the wild leader of a herd sometimes turning his fine head to one side to look back at the master or gaze over the hills, sometimes slackening to a trot up a sharper ascent or lengthening into a fuller gallop on an easy down-slope. There seemed no purpose in the reins which were kept just taut enough to give the rider the feel of his mount, and the left hand which held them was never still for a moment, but played back and forth slightly with the motion of the head. Except in times of crisis those reins were not for the transmission of orders, it seemed, but they served as the wires through which the mind of the man and the mind of the horse kept in telegraphic touch.

In the meantime Black Bart loafed behind, lingering on the crest of each rise to look back, and then racing to catch up, but halfway back to Rickett he came up beside the master, whining, and leaping as high as Barry's knee.

"You seen something?" queried Barry. "Are they comin' on the trail again?"

He swayed a bit to one side and diverted Satan out of his course so as to climb one of the more commanding swells. From this point he glanced back and saw a dust cloud, much like that which a small whirlwind picks up, rolling down the nearest slope of the Morgan Hills.

At that distance the posse looked hardly larger than one unit, and certainly they could not see the single horseman they followed; however, they could follow the trail easily across this ground. Satan had turned to look back.

"Shall we go back and play around 'em, boy?" asked Barry.

Black Bart had run on ahead, and now he turned with a short howl.

"The partner says 'no,'" continued the master. "Of all the dogs I ever see, Bart plays the most careful game, but out on the trail, Satan"—here he sent the stallion in to the sweeping lope—"Bart knows more'n you an' me put together, so we'll do what he says."

For answer, Satan lengthened a little into his stride. As for the wolf-dog, he went off like a black bolt into the eye of the wind, streaking it west to hunt out the easiest course. A wolf,—and surely there was more of wolf than of dog in Black Bart—has a finer sense for the lay of ground than anything on four feet. He knows how to come down the wind on his quarry keeping to the depressions and ravines so that not a taint of his presence is blown to the prey; and he will skulk across an open plain, stealing from hollow to hollow and stalking from bush to bush, so that the wariest are taken by surprise. As for Black Bart, he knew the kind of going which the stallion liked as well, almost, as he knew his own preferences, and he picked out a course which a surveyor with line and spirit-level could hardly have bettered. He wove across the country in loosely thrown semicircles, and came back in view of the master at the proper point. There was hardly much point in such industry in a country as smooth as this, not much more difference, say, than the saving of distance which the horse makes who hugs the fence on the turn and on account of that sticks his head under the finish wire a nose in front; and Bart clung to his work with scrupulous care.

Sometimes he ran back with lolling, red tongue, when the course lay clear even to the duller sense of a human, and frisked under the nose of Satan until a word from Barry sent him scurrying away like a pleased child. His duties comprehended not only the selection of the course

181

but also an eagle vigilance before and behind, so that when he came again with a peculiar whine, Barry leaned a little from the saddle and spoke to him anxiously.

"D'you mean to say that they been gainin' ground on us old boy?"

Black Bart leaped sidewise, keeping his head toward the master, and he howled in troubled fashion.

"Whereaway are they now?" muttered Barry, and looked back again.

A great distance behind, hardly distinguishable now, the dust of the posse was blending into the landscape and losing itself against a gray background.

"If they's nothin' wrong behind, what's bitin' you, Bart. You gettin' hungry, maybe? Want to hurry home?"

Another howl, still louder, answered him.

"Go on, then, and show me where they's trouble."

Black Bart whirled and darted off almost straight ahead, but bearing up a hill slightly south of their course. Toward the top of this eminence he changed his lope for a skulking trot that brought his belly fur trailing on the ground.

"They's somethin' *ahead* of us, Satan!" cried the master softly. "What could that be? It's men, by the way Bart sneaks up to look at 'em. They's nothin' else that he'd do that way for. Easy, boy, and go soft!"

The stallion cut his gallop into a slinking trot, his head lowered, even his ears flat back, and glided up the hillside. Barry swung to the ground and crawled to the top of the hill. What he saw was a dozen mounted men swinging down into the low, broad scoop of ground beyond the hill. They raced with their hatbrims standing stiff up in the wind.

"They've been watchin' us with glasses!" whispered Dan to Bart, and the wolf-dog snarled savagely, his neck-fur ruffling up.

The dozen directly in front were not all, for to the right, bearing straight across his original course, came another group almost as strong, and to the left eight more riders spurred at top speed.

"We almost walked into 'em," said Barry, "but they ain't got us yet. Back, boy!"

The wolf dog slunk down the hill until it was out of

sight from the farther side of the slope, and the master imitated these tactics until he was close to Satan. Once in the saddle he made up his mind quickly. Someone in Rickett had guessed his intention to double back toward Tucker Creek, and they had cut him off cleverly enough and in overwhelming force. However, no one in Rickett could guess that another way out remained for him in the fords below Caswell City, and even if they knew, their knowledge would do them no good. They could not wing a message to that place to head him off! it was not humanly possible. For Dan knew nothing of the telephone lines which brought Caswell City itself within speaking distance of far away Rickett. Caswell City, then, was his goal, but to get toward it he must circle far back toward the Morgan Hills, back almost into the teeth of the posse in order to skirt around the right wing of these new enemies. Even then, to double that flank, he must send Satan ahead at full speed. As he swung around, the eight men of that end party crashed over the hill five hundred yards away, and their yell at the view of the quarry went echoing up the shallow valley.

The slayer of Pete Glass, he who had done the notorious Killing at Alder, was almost in touch of their revolvers—and their horses were fresh. Not one of that eight but would have given odds on his chances of sharing the capture money. There were no spurs on the heels of Barry to urge Satan, and no quirt in his hand, but a single word sent the black streaking down the hill.

Going into the Morgan Hills he had gone like the wind, but now he rushed like a thoroughbred standing a challenge in the homestretch. His nose, and his flying tail were a straight line and the flash of his legs was a tangle which no eye could follow as he shot east on the back trail, straight toward the posse. For a mile or more that speed did not slacken, and at the end of that distance he began to edge to the right.

The men behind him knew well enough what the plan of the fugitive was, and they angled farther toward the north; there in the distance came the posse, the cloud of dust breaking up now into the dark figures of the fifteen, and if the men from St. Vincent could hold the pace a little longer they would drive Barry between two fires. They flattened themselves along their horses' necks at infinite risk of their necks in case of a stumble, and every spur in the crowd was dripping red; horseflesh could do no more, and still the black drew ahead inches and inches with every stride.

If they could not turn him with their speed another way remained, and by swift agreement the four best horses were sent ahead at full speed while the other riders caught their reins over the pommels and jerked out their rifles; a quartet of bullets went screaming after the black horse.

Indeed, there was little enough chance that a placed shot would go home, but their magazines were full, and a chance hit would do the work and kill both man and horse at that rate of speed. Dan Barry knew it, and when the bullets sang he whirled in the saddle and swept out his rifle from its case in the same movement. That yellow devil of anger flared in his eyes as he pitched the butt to his shoulder and straight into the circle of the sight rode Johnny Gasney of St. Vincent. Another volley whistled about him and his finger trembled on the trigger. No chance work with Barry, for he knew the gait of Satan as a practiced naval gunner knows the swing of his ship in a smooth sea, and that circle of doom wavered over Johnny Gasney for a dozen strides before Dan turned with a faint moan and jammed the rifle back in its case. Once again he was balancing in his stirrups, leaning close to cut the wind with his shoulders.

"I can't do it, Satan. I got nothin' agin them. They think they're playin' square. I can't do it. Stretch out, old boy. Stretch out!"

It seemed impossible that the stallion could increase his exertions, but with that low voice at his ear he did literally stretch along the ground and jerked himself away from the pursuit like a tall ship when a new sail spreads in a gale.

The men from St. Vincent saw that the game was lost. Every one of the eight had his rifle at the shoulder and the bullets hissed everywhere about him. Right into his face, but a greater distance away, rode the posse from

Rickett, the fifteen tried men and true; and having caught the scheme of the trap they were killing their horses with a last effort.

It failed through no fault of theirs. Just as the jaws of the trap were about to close the black stallion whisked out from danger, lunged over a swell of ground, and was out of view. When they reached that point, yelling, Barry raced his black out of range of all except the wildest chance shot. The eight from St. Vincent drove their weapons sullenly into the holsters; for the last five minutes they had been silently dividing ten thousand dollars by eight, and the awakening left a taste of ashes.

They could only follow him now at a moderate pace in the hope of wearing him down, and since a slight pause made little difference in the result—it would even be an advantage to breathe their horses after that burst,—they drew rein and cursed in chorus.

CHAPTER XXXII

Relays

The horses from St. Vincent already wheezed from the run, but the mounts of the posse were staggering—completely blown. Ever since they left Rickett they had been going at close to top speed and the last rush finished them; at least seven of that chosen fifteen would never be worth their salt again, and they stood with hanging heads, bloody foam upon their breasts and dripping from their mouths, their sides laboring, and breathing with that rattle which the rider dreads. The posse, to a man, swung sullenly to the ground.

"Who's boss, boys?" called Johnny Gasney, puffing in his saddle as he rode up. "By God, we'll get him yet! They's a devil in that black hoss! Who's boss?"

"I ain't exactly boss," answered Mark Retherton, whom not even fear of death could hurry in his ways of speech, "but maybe I can talk for the boys. What you want, Johnny?"

"You gents'll be needin' new hosses?"

"We'll be needin' graves for the ones we got," growled Mark, and he stared gloomily at the dull eye of his pinto. "The best cuttin' out hoss I ever throwed a leg over, and now—look at him!"

"Here's your relay!" cut in Johnny Gasney. "Old Billy 'phoned down." Five men came leading three spare horses apiece. "He phoned down and asked me to get fifteen hosses ready. He must of guessed where Barry would head. And here they are—the best ponies in St. Vincent—but for God's sake use 'em better'n you did that set!"

The other members of the posse set to work silently changing their saddles to the new relay, and Mark Retherton tossed his answer over his shoulder to Johnny Gasney while he drew his cinch brutally tight.

"They's a pile of hoss-flesh in these parts, but they ain't more'n one Barry. You gents can say good-by to your hosses unless we nail him before they're run down."

Johnny Gasney rubbed his red, fat forehead, perplexed.

"It's all right," he decided, "because it ain't possible the black hoss can outlast these. But—he sure seemed full of runnin! One thing more, Mark. You don't need to fear pressin' Barry, because he won't shoot. He had his gun out, but I guess he don't want to run up his score any higher'n it is. He put it back without firin' a shot. Go on, boys, and go like hell. Billy has lined up a new relay for you at Wago."

They made no pause to start in a group, but each sent home the spurs as soon as he was in the saddle. They had ridden for the blood of Pete Glass before, but now at least seven of them rode for the sake of the horses they had ruined, and to a cow-puncher a favorite mount is as dear as a friend.

They expected to find the black out of sight, but it was a welcome surprise to see him not half a mile away wading across St. Vincent Creek; for Barry quite accurately guessed that there would be a pause in the pursuit after that hair-breadth escape, and at the creek he stopped to let Satan get his wind. He would not trust the stallion to drink, but gave him a bare mouthful from his hat and loosened the cinches for an instant.

Not that this was absolutely necessary, for Satan was neither blown nor leg-weary. He stood dripping with sweat, indeed, but poised lightly, his head high, his ears pricked, his nostrils distended to transparency as he drew in great breaths. Even that interval Barry used, for he set to work vigorously massaging the muscles of shoulders and hips and whipping off the sweat from neck and flank. It was several moments, and already Satan's breath came easily, when Black Bart shot down from his watch-post and warned them on with a snarl, but still, before he tightened the cinches again and climbed to the saddle Barry took the fine head of the stallion between his hands.

"Between you and me, Satan," he murmured, "our day's work is jest beginnin'. Are you feelin' fit?"

Satan nuzzled the shoulder of the master and snorted his answer; Black Bart had given the warning, and the stallion was eager to be off.

They crossed the creek at a place where the stones came almost to the surface, since nothing is more detrimental to the speed of a horse than a plunge in cold water, and with the hoofbeats of the posse growing up behind they cantered off again a little east of north, straight for Caswell City.

There was little work for Black Bart in such country as this, for there was rarely a rise of ground over which a man on horseback could not look, and the surface was race-track fast. Once Satan knew the direction there was nothing for it but to sit the saddle and let him work, and he fell into his long-distance gait. It was a smart pace for any ordinary animal to follow through half a day's journey, and Barry knew with perfect certainty that there was not the slightest chance of even the fresh horses behind him wearing down Satan before night; but to his astonishment the trailers rode as if they had limitless horseflesh at their command. Perhaps they were unaware of the running that was still in Satan, so Barry sent the stallion on at a free gallop that shunted the sagebrush past him in a dizzy whirl.

A mile of this, but when he looked back the posse were even closer. They were riding still with the spur! It was madness, but it was not his part to worry for them, and it was necessary that he maintain at least this interval, so he leaned a little forward to cut the wind more easily, and Satan leaped into a faster pace. He had several distinct advantages over the mounts of the posse. At their customary rolling lope they will travel all day with hardly a break, but they have neither the size nor the length of leg for sustained bursts of speed. Moreover, most of the cowponies who now raced on the trail of Satan carried riders who outweighed Barry by twenty pounds and in addition to this they were burdened by saddles made ponderously to stand the strain of roping cattle, whereas Barry's specially made saddle was hardly half that weight.

Perhaps more than all this, the cowponies rode by compulsion, urged with sharp spurs, checked and guided by the jaw-breaking curb, whereas Satan frolicked along at his own will, or at least at the will of a master which was one with his. No heavy bit worried his mouth, no pointed steel tormented his flanks. He had only one handicap—the weight of his rider, and that weight was balanced and distributed with the care of a perfect horseman.

With all this in mind it was hardly wonderful that the stallion kept the posse easily in play. His breathing was a trifle harder, now, and perhaps there was not quite the same light spring in his gallop, but Barry looking back, could tell by the tossing heads of the horses which followed that they were being quickly run down to the last gasp. Mile after mile there was not a pause in that murderous pace, and then, cutting the sky with a row of sharply pointed roofs, he saw a town straight ahead and groaned in understanding.

It was rather new country to Barry, but the possse must know it like a book. They were spending their horses freely because they hoped to arrange for a fresh series of mounts in Wago. However, it would take some time for them to arrange the details of the loan, and by that time he would be out of sight among the hills which stretched ahead. That would give him a sufficient start, and he would make the fords near Caswell City comfortably ahead. At Caswell City, indeed, they might get a still other relay, but just beyond the Asper River rose the Grizzly Peaks—his own country, and once among them he could laugh the posse to scorn.

He patted Satan on the shoulder and swept on at redoubled speed, skirting close to the town, while the posse plunged straight into it.

Listening closely, he could hear their shouts as they entered the village, could mark the cessation of their hoof-beats.

Ten minutes, five minutes at least for the change of horses, and that time would put him safely among the hills.

But the impossible happened. There was no pause of minutes, hardly a pause of seconds, when the rush of hoofbeats began again and poured out from the town, fifteen desperate riders on fifteen fresh mounts. By some miracle Wago had been warned and the needed horses had been kept there saddled and ready for the relay.

It turned an easy escape in a close chance, but still his faith in Satan was boundless to reach the fords in time, and the safety of the mountains beyond. Another word, and with a snort the great-hearted stallion swept up the slope, with Black Bart at his old work, skirting ahead and choosing the easiest way. That was another great handicap in favor of the fugitive, and every advantage counted with redoubled significance now, every foot of distance saved, every inch of climb avoided.

A new obstacle confronted him, for the low, rolling hills were everywhere checkered with squares and oblongs of plowed ground, freshly turned, and guarded by tall fences of barbed-wire. They could be jumped, but jumping was no easy matter for a tiring horse, and Barry saw, with a sigh of relief, a sharp gulch to the left which cut straight through that region of broken farms and headed north and east pointing like an arrow in the direction of the fords. He swung down into it without a thought and pressed on. The bottom was gravelly, here and there, from the effect of the waters which had once washed through the ravine and cut these sides so straight, but over the greater part of the bottom sand had drifted, and the going was hardly worse than the hilly stretches above.

The sides grew higher, now, with great rapidity. Already they were up to the shoulder of Satan, now up to his withers, and from behind the roar of the posse racing at full speed, filled the gulch with confusion of echoes. They must be racing their horses as if they were entering the homestretch, as if they were sure of the goal. It was strange.

CHAPTER XXXIII

The Jump

He brought Satan back to a hand canter, and so he pulled around the next curve of the gulch and saw the trap squarely in front. He came to a full halt. For he saw a tall, strong barbed-wire fence stretching across the stream-bed, and beyond the fence were a litter of chicken-coops, iron bands from broken barrels and a thousand other of those things which brand the typical western farm-yard; above the top of the bank to his left he caught a glimpse of the sharp roof of the house.

He looked back, but it was far too late to turn, ride down the ravine to a place where the bank could be scaled, and cut across country once more. The posse came like a whirlwind, yelling, shooting as if they hoped to at-tract attention, and attention they certainly won, for now Dan saw a tall middle-aged fellow, his long beard blowing over one shoulder as he ran, come down into the farm-yard with a double-barreled shotgun in his hands. He was a type of those who do not know what it is to miss their target—probably because ammunition comes so high; and with a double load of buckshot it was literally death to come within his range. Dan knew that a great many chances may be taken against a revolver and even a rifle can be tricked, but it is suicide to flirt with a shotgun in the hands of one used to bring down doves as they sloped out of the air toward a water-hole. The farmer stood with his broad-brimmed straw hat pushed far back on his head looking up and down the ravine, a perfect target—and Barry's hand slipped automatically over his rifle.

His fingers refused to close upon it.

"I can't do it, Satan," he whispered. "We got to take

our chances of gettin' by, that's all. *He* didn't have no hand with Grey Molly."

Narrow chances indeed, by this time, for the brief pause had brought the posse fairly upon his heels; the farmer saw the fugitive and brought his shotgun to the ready; and Black Bart in an agony of impatience raced round and round the master. A wild cheer rose from the posse and came echoing about him; they had sighted their quarry. From Rickett to Morgan Hills, from Morgan Hills to St. Vincent, from St. Vincent to Wago and far beyond; but this was the end of an historic run.

"D'ye see?" whispered Barry, leaning close to Satan's ears. "Lad, d'ye see what you've got to do?"

The black stood with his head very high, quivering through his whole body while he eyed the fence. It was murderously high, and all things were against him, the long run, the rise of the ground going toward the fence, and the gravel from which he must take off for the jump.

"You can do it," said the master. "You *got* to do it! Go for it, boy. We win or lose together!"

He swayed forward, and Satan leaped ahead at full speed, gathering impetus, scattering the gravel on either side. The farmer on the inside of the fence raised his shotgun leisurely to his shoulder and took careful aim. He knew what it all meant. He had heard of the outlaw, Barry, with his black-horse and his wolf-dog—everyone in the desert had, for that matter—and even had he been ignorant the shouting of the posse which now raced down the canyon in full view would have told him all that he needed to know. How many things went through his mind while he squinted down the gleaming barrel! He thought of the long labor on the farm and the mortgage which still ate the life of his produce every year; he thought of the narrow bowed shoulders of his wife; he thought of the meager faces of his children; and he thought first and last of ten thousand dollars reward! No wonder the hand which supported the barrels was steady as an iron prop. He was shooting for his life and the happiness of five souls!

He would save his fire till he literally saw the white of the enemy's eyes: until the outlaw reached the fence. No horse on the mountain-desert could top that highest strand of wire as he very well knew; and in his youth, back in Kentucky, he had ridden hunters. That fence came exactly to the top of his head, and the top of his head was six feet and two inches from the ground. To make assurance doubly sure he dropped upon one knee and made that shotgun an unstirring part and portion of himself.

Nobly, nobly the black came on, his ears pricking as he judged the great task and his head carried a little high and back as any good jumper knows his head must be carried.

The practiced eye of the farmer watched the outlaw gather his horse under him. Well he knew the meaning of that shortening grip on the reins to give the horse the last little lift that might mean success or failure in the jump. Well he knew that rise in the stirrups, that leaning forward, and his heart rose in unison and went back to the blue grass of Kentucky glittering in the sun.

Before them went the wolf-dog, skimming low, reached the fence, and shot over it in a graceful, high-arched curve.

Then the shout of the rider: "Up! *Up!*"

And the stallion reared and leaped. He seemed to graze it coming up, so close was his take-off; he seemed to be pawing his way over with the forefeet; and then with both legs doubled close, hugging his body, he shot across and left the highest strand of the wire quivering and humming.

The farmer hurled his best shotgun a dozen yards away and threw up his hat.

"Go it, lad! God bless ye; and good luck!"

The hand of the rider lifted in mute acknowledgment, and as he shot past, the farmer caught a glimpse of a delicately handsome face that smiled down at him.

"The left gate! The left gate!" he shouted through his cupped hands, and as the fugitive rushed through the upper gate he turned to face the posse which was already pulling up at the fence and drawing their wire-cutters.

As Barry shot out onto the higher ground on the other side of the farmhouse he could see them severing the wires and the interruption of the chase would be only a matter

193

of seconds. But seconds counted triply now, and the halt and the time they would spend getting up impetus all told in favor of the fugitive.

Thirty-five miles, or thereabouts, since they left Rickett that morning, and still the black ran smoothly, with a lilt to his gallop. Dan Barry lifted his head and his whistling soared and pulsed and filled the air. It made Bart come back to him; it made Satan toss his head and glance at the master from the corner of his bright eye, for this was an assurance that the battle was over and the rest not far away.

On they drove, straight as a bird flies for Caswell City, and Black Bart, ranging ahead among the hills, was picking the way once more. If the stallion were tired, he gave no sign of it. The sweep of his stride brushed him past rocks and shrubs, and he literally flowed uphill and down, far different from the horses which scampered in his rear, for they pounded the earth with their efforts, grunting under the weight of fifty pound saddles and heavy riders. Another handicap checked them, for while Satan ran on alone, freely, the bunched pursuers kept a continual friction back and forth. The leaders reined in to keep back with the mass of the posse, and those in the rear by dint of hard spurring would rush up to the front in turn until some spirited nag challenged for the lead, so that there was a steady interplay among the fifteen. Their gait at the best could not be more than the pace of their slowest member, but even that pace was diminished by the difficulties of group riding. Yet Mark Retherton refused to allow his men to scatter and stretch out. He kept them in hand steadily, a bunched unit ready to strike together, for he had seen the dead body of Pete Glass and he kept in mind a picture of what might happen if this fellow should whirl and pick off the posse man by man. Better prolong the run, for in the end no single horse could stand up against so many relays. Yet it was maddening to watch the stallion float over hill and dale with that same unbroken stride.

Once and again he sent the fresh horses from Wago after the fugitive in a sprinting burst, but each time the black drifted farther away, and mile after mile Mark

Retherton pulled his field glasses to his eyes and strained his vision to make out some sign of labor in the gait of Satan. There was no change. His head was still high, the rhythm of his lope unfaltering.

But here the Wago Mountains—not more than ragged hills, to be sure—cut across the path of the outlaw and in those hills, unless the message which waited for him at Wago had been false, should be the men of Caswell City, two score or more besides the fifteen fresh horses for the posse. Two score of men, at least, Caswell could send out, and from the heights they could surely detect the coming of Barry and plant themselves in his way. An ambush, a volley, would end this famous ride.

The hills came up on them swiftly, now, and if the men of Caswell failed in their duty it meant safety for the fugitive, because two miles beyond were the willows of the marshes and fords across the Asper River. There could only be two alternatives, since not a man showed on the hills. Either they waited in ambush, or else they had mistaken the route along which Barry would come, and the latter was hardly possible. With his glasses Mark Retherton scanned the hills anxiously and it was then that he saw the dark form of the wolf-dog skulking on before the outlaw. He had watched Black Bart before this, of course, but never with suspicion until he noted the peculiar manner in which the animal skirted here and there through the rough ground, pausing on high places, weaving back and forth across the course of his master.

"Like a scout," thought Retherton. "And by God, there he comes to report!"

For Black Bart had whirled and raced straight back for Dan. There was no need of howl or whine to give the reason of his coming; the speed of his running meant business, and Barry shortened the pace of Satan while he looked over the hills, incredulous, despairing. It could not be that men lurked there to cut him off. No living thing could have raced from Rickett to Caswell City to warn them of his coming. Nevertheless, there came Bart with the ill tidings, and it only remained to skirt swiftly east, round the dangerous ground, and strike the marshes first.

He swung Satan around on the new course with a pressure of his knees and loosed him into a freer gallop.

They must have sensed the meaning of this maneuver at once, for hardly had he stretched out east when voices shouted out of the hills, and around and over several low knolls came forty horsemen, racing. Half a dozen were already due east—no escape that way; and the long line of the others came straight at him with the slope of the ground to give them velocity.

CHAPTER XXXIV

The Warning

All in a grim instant he saw the trap. It closed upon his consciousness with a click, and as he doubled Satan around he knew that the only escape was in running southeast along the banks of the Asper. Even that was a desperate, a forlorn chance, for if that omnipotent voice could reach from Rickett to Caswell City, fifty miles away, certainly it must have warned the river towns of Ganton and Wilsonville and Bly Falls where Tucker Creek ran into the Asper. But this was no time for thinking. Already, looking back, he saw the posse changing their saddles to fifteen fresh mounts, and he headed Satan across the Wago Hills, West and South.

It was hot work. Even the steel-wire muscles of Black Bart were weakening under the tremendous labors of that day, and as he scouted ahead his head was low and his red tongue lolled, and surest sign of all, the bushy tail drooped; yet it was time to make a new call upon both wolf-dog and horse, for the posse was racing after him as before, giving even the fresh, willing mounts the urge of spurs and quirts. He ran his hand down the dripping neck and shoulder of Satan; he called to him; and with a snort the stallion responded. He felt the quiver as the muscles tightened for the work; he felt the settling as Satan lengthened to racing speed.

Through the Wago Hills, then, with Bart picking the way as before, and never a falter in the sweep of Satan's running. If his head was a little lower, if his ears lay flat, only the master knew the meaning, and still, when he spoke, the glistening ears pricked up, and they bounded on to a greater speed than before. The flight of a gull on

197

unstirring wings when the wind buoys it, the glide of water over the descent of smooth rock, with never a ripple, like all things effortless, swift, and free, such was the gait of Satan as he fled. Let them spur the fresh horses from Caswell City till their flanks dripped red, they would never gain on him.

On through the hills, and now the heave of his great breaths told of the strain, down like an arrow into the rolling ground, and now they galloped beside the Asper banks. The master looked darkly upon that water.

Ten days before, when the snows had not yet reached the climax of melting, ten days later when that climax was overpassed, the Asper would have been fordable, but now a brown flood stormed along the gully, ate away the banks, undermined the willows here and there, and rolled stones larger than a man could lift. It went with an angry shouting as if it defied the fugitive. It was narrow, maddeningly narrow, almost small enough to attempt a leap across to the safety of the thickets on the farther side, but the force of the water alone was enough to warn the bravest swimmer away, and here and there, like teeth in the mouth of the shark, jagged stones cut the surface with white foam streaking out below them; as if to prove its power, even while Dan turned South along the bank a dead trunk shot down the stream and split on one of the Asper's teeth.

Even then he felt the temptation. There lay the forest on the farther side, a forest which would shelter him, and above the forest, hardly a mile back, began the Grizzly Peaks. They lunged straight up to snowy summits, and all along their sides blue shadows of the afternoon drifted through a network of ravines—a promise of peace, a surety of safety if he could reach that labyrinth.

He was almost glad when he left the mockery of the river's noise to turn aside for Ganton. There it lay in the bend of the Asper in the low-lands, and every town where men lived was an enemy. He could see them now gathered just outside the village, twenty men, perhaps and fifteen spare horses, the best they had, for the posse.

On past Ganton, and again a call upon Satan to meet the first spurt of the posse on its new horses. There was something in the stallion to answer, some incredible reserve of nerve strength and courage. There was a slight labor, now, and something of the same heave and pitch which comes in the gait of a common horse; also, when he put Satan up the first slope beyond Ganton he noted a faltering, a deeper lowering of the head. When his hoofs struck a loose rock he no longer had the easy recoil of the morning. He staggered like a graceful yacht chopped by a cross-current. Now down the slope, now back to the roar of the Asper once more, for there the going was most level, but always the strides were shortening, shortening, and the head of the stallion nodded at his work.

All that was seen by Mark Retherton through his glasses, though they were almost close enough now to see details through the naked eye. He turned in the saddle to the posse, grim faces, sweat and dust clotted in their moustaches, their faces drawn and gray with streaks over the nose and under the eyes where perspiration ran. They rode crookedly, now, for seventy miles at full speed had racked them, twisted them, cramped their muscles. Scotty kept his head tilted far back, for his spinal column seemed about to snap. Walsh leaned to his right side which a tormenting pain drew at every stride, and Hendricks cursed in gasps through a wry mouth.

It had been an hour since Mark Retherton last spoke, and when he attempted it now his voice was as hoarse as a croaking frog.

"Boys, buck up! He's done! D'ye see the black laborin'. D'ye see it? Hey, Lew, Garry, we've got the best hosses among us three. Now's the time for a spurt, and by God, we'll run him down. I'm startin'!"

He made his word good with an Indian yell and a wave of his hat that sent his buckskin leaping straight into the air, to land with stiff legs, "swallowing its head," but then it straightened out in earnest. That buckskin had a name from Bly Falls to Caswell City for speed and courage, and it lived up to the record in this time of need. Close behind it came Lew and Garry on ponies scarcely slower than the buckskin, and they closed rapidly on Satan. The plan of Retherton was plain. Now that the black was running on its nerve a spurt might bring them within striking distance and if they could check the flight for an instant by opening advance guard fire, they might drive the fugitive into a corner by the river and hold him there until the main body of the posse came up. The three of them running alone in the lead could do five yards for every four of the slower horses, and the effect showed at once.

Going up a slope the trot of the stallion maintained or even increased his lead, but when they reached the easier ground beyond they drew rapidly upon him. They saw Barry bend low; they saw the stallion increase its pace.

"By God," shouted Retherton in involuntary admiration, "I'd rather have that hoss than the ten thousand. But feed 'em the spurs, boys, and he'll come back to us inside a mile."

And Retherton was right. Before that mile was out the black slipped back inch by inch, until at length Retherton called: "Now grab your guns, partners, and see if you can salt him down with lead. Give your hosses' their heads and turn loose!"

They pulled their guns to their shoulders and sent a volley at the outlaw. One bullet clipped a spark from the rocks just behind the stallion's feet; the other two must have gone wide. Once more Barry flinched closer over the neck of Satan and once again the horse answered with a fresh burst of speed, but in a few moments he came back to them. Flesh could not stand that pace after seventy-five miles of running.

They saw the rider straighten and look back; then the sun flashed on his rifle.

"Feed 'em the spur!" shouted Retherton. "If we can't hit him shooting ahead, he ain't got a chance to hit us shootin' backwards." For it is notoriously hard to turn in the saddle and accomplish anything with a rifle. One is moving away from the target instead of toward it, and every condition of ordinary shooting is reversed; above all, the moment a man turns his head he is completely out of touch with his horse. Apparently the fugitive knew this and made no attempt to place his shots. He merely jerked his gun to the shoulder and blazed away as soon as it was in place;

half a dozen yards in front of Retherton the bullet kicked up the dust.

"I told you," he shouted. "He can't do nothin' that way. Close in, boys. Close in for God's sake!"

He himself was flailing with his quirt, and the buckskin grunted at every strike. Once more the rifle pitched to the outlaw's shoulder, and this time the bullet clicked on a rock not ten feet from Retherton, and again on a straight line for him.

"Damned if that ain't shootin'!" called Garry, and Retherton, alarmed, swung the buckskin out to one side to throw the marksman out of line. He had turned again in the saddle, and as though the episode were at an end, restored his rifle to its case, but when they poured in another volley about him, he swung sharply roundabout again, gun in hand. Once more the rifle went to his shoulder, and this time the bullet knocked a puff of dust into the very nostrils of the buckskin. Retherton reined in with an oath.

"He's been warnin' me boys," he called. "That devil has the range like he was sitting in a rockin'chair shooting at a tin-can. He's warnin' us back to the rest of the gang. And damned if we ain't goin'!"

It was quite patent that he was right, for three bullets sent on a line for one horse, and each of them closer, could mean only one thing. They checked their horses, and in a moment the rest of the posse was clattering around them.

"It don't make no difference," called Retherton, "savin' in time. Maybe he'll last to Wilsonville, but he can't stay in three miles when we hang onto him with fresh hosses. The black is runnin' on nothin' but guts right now."

CHAPTER XXXV

The Asper

Ninety miles of ground, at least, had been covered by the black stallion, since he left Rickett that morning, yet when he galloped across the plain in full sight of Wilsonville there were plenty of witnesses who vowed that Satan ran like a colt frolicking over a pasture. Mark Retherton knew better, and the posse to a man felt the end was near. They changed saddles in a savage silence and went down the street out of town with a roar of racing hoofs.

And Barry too, as he watched them whip around the corner of the last house and streak across the fields, knew that the end of the ride was near. Strength, wind and nerve were gone from Satan; his hoofs pounded the ground with the stamp of a plowhorse; his breath came in wheezes with a rattle toward the end; the tail no longer fluttered out straight behind. Yet when the master leaned and called he found something in his great heart with which to answer. A ghost of his old buoyancy came in his stride, the drooping head rose, one ear quivered up, and he ran against the challenge of those fresh ponies from Wilsonville. There were men who doubted it when the tale was told, but Mark Retherton swore to the truth of it.

Even then that desperate effort was failing. Not all the generous will in the heart of the stallion could give his legs the speed they needed; and he fell back by inches, by feet, by yards, toward the posse. They disdained their guns now, and kept them in the cases; for the game was theirs.

And then they noted an odd activity in the fugitive, who had slipped to one side and was fumbling at his cinches. They could not understand for a time, but presently the saddle came loose, the cinches flipped out, and the whole apparatus crashed to the ground. Nor was this all. The rider leaned forward and his hands worked on the head of his mount until the hackamore also came free and was tossed aside. To that thing fifteen good men and true swore the next day with strange oaths, and told how a man rode for his life on a horse that wore neither saddle nor bridle but ran obediently to voice and hand.

Every ounce counted, and there were other ounces to be spared. He was leaning again, to this side and then to that, and presently the posse rushed past the discarded riding-boots.

There lay the rifle in its case on the saddle far behind. And with the rifle remained all the fugitive's chances of fighting at long range. Now, following, came the heavy cartridge belt and the revolver with it. The very sombrero was torn from his head and thrown away.

His horse was failing visibly—not even this lightening could keep it away from the posse long; and yet the man threw away his sole chance of safety. And the fifteen pursuers cursed solemnly as they saw the truth. He would run his horse to death and then die with it empty handed rather than let either of them fall a captive.

Unburdened by saddle or gun or trapping, the stallion gave himself in the last effort. There ahead lay safety, if they could shake off this last relay of the posse, and for a time he pulled away until Retherton grew anxious, and once more the bullets went questing around the fugitive. But it was a dying effort. They gained; they drew away; and then they were only holding the posse even, and then once more, they fell back gradually toward the pursuit. It was the end, and Barry sat bolt erect and looked around him; that would be the last of him and the last scene he should see.

There came the posse, distant but running closer. With every stride Satan staggered; with every stride his head drooped, and all the lilt of his running was gone. Ten minutes, five minutes more and the fifteen would be around him. He looked to the river which thundered there at his side.

It was the very swiftest portion of all the Asper between Tucker Creek and Caswell City. Even at that moment, a few hundred yards away, a tall tree which had been undermined, fell into the stream and dashed the spray high; yet even that fall was silent in the general roar of the river. Checked by the body and the branches of the tree for an instant before it should be torn away from the bank and shot down stream, the waters boiled and left a comparatively smooth, swift sliding current beyond the obstruction; and it gave to Barry a chance or a ghost of a chance:

The central portion of the river bed was chopped with sharp rocks which tore the stream into white rags of foam; but beyond these rocks, a little past the middle, the tree like a dam smoothed out the current; it was still swift but not torn with swirls or cross-currents, and in that triangle of comparatively still water of which the base was the fallen tree, the apex lay on a sand bar, jutting a few yards from the bank. And the forlorn hope of Barry was to swing the stallion a little distance away from the banks, run him with the last of his ebbing strength straight for the bank, and try to clear the rocky portion of the river bed with a long leap that might, by the grace of God, shoot him into the comparatively protected current. Even then it would be a game only a tithe won, for the chances were ten to one that before they could struggle close to the shore, the currents would suck them out toward the center. They would never reach that shelving bit of sand, but the sharp rocks of the stream would tear them a moment later like teeth. Yet the dimmest chance was a good chance now.

He called Satan away from his course, and at the change of direction the stallion staggered, but went on, turned at another call, and headed straight for the stream. He was blind with running; he was numbed by the long horror of that effort, no doubt, but there was enough strength left in him to understand the master's mind. He tossed his head high, he flaunted out his tail, and sped with a ghost of his old sweeping gallop toward the bank.

"Bart!" shouted the master, and waved his arm.

And the wolf saw too. He seemed to cringe for a moment, and then, like some old leader of a pack who knows he is about to die and defies his death, he darted for the river and flung himself through the air.

An instant later Satan reared on the bank and shot into the air. Below him the teeth of the rocks seemed to lift up in hunger, and the white foam jumped to take him. The crest of the arc of his jump was passed; he shot lower, and grazing the last of the stones he plunged out of sight in the swift water beyond. There were two falls, not one, for even while the black was in the air Barry slipped from his back and struck the water clear of Satan.

They came up again struggling in the last effort toward the shore. The impetus of their leap had washed them well in toward the bank, but the currents dragged them out again toward the center of the stream where the rocks waited. Down river they went, and Black Bart alone had a ghost of a chance for success. His leap had been farther and he skimmed the surface when he struck so that by dint of fierce swimming he hugged close to the shore, and then his claws bedded in the sand-bank.

As for Barry, the waters caught him and sent him spinning over and over, like a log, whipping down stream while the heavier body of Satan was struggling whole yards above. There was no chance for the master to reach the sand-bank, and even if he reached it he could not cling; but the wolf-dog knew many things about water. In the times of famine long years before the days of the master there had been ways of catching fish.

He edged forwards until the water foamed about his shoulders. Down came Dan, his arms tumbling as he whirled, and on the sleeve of one of those arms the teeth of Bart closed. The cloth was stout, and yet it ripped as if it were rotten veiling, and the tug nearly swept Bart from his place. Still, he clung; his teeth shifted their hold with the speed of light and closed over the arm of the master itself, slipped, sank deeper, drew blood, and held. Barry swung around and a moment later stood with his feet buried firmly in the bank.

He had not a moment to spare, for Satan, only his eyes and his nose showing, rushed down the current, making his last fight. Barry thrust his feet deeper in the sand, leaned, buried both hands in the mane of the stallion. It was a far fiercer tug-of-war this time, for the ample body of the horse gave the water a greater surface to grapple on, yet the strength of the man sufficed. His back bowed; his shoulders ached with the strain; and then the fore-feet of Satan pawed the sand, and all three staggered up the shelving bank, reeled among the trees, and collapsed in safety.

So great was the roar of the water that they heard neither shouts nor the reports of the guns, but for several minutes the bullets of the posse combed the shrubbery as high as the breast of a man.

CHAPTER XXXVI

The Empty Cave

Through ten months of the year a child of ten could wade the Asper but now its deep roaring that set the ground quivering under Barry gave him perfect assurance of safety. Not one of that posse would attempt the crossing, he felt, but he slipped back through the shrubbery close to the bank to make sure. He was in time to see Mark Retherton give a command with gestures that sent reluctant guns into the holsters. Fists were brandished toward the green covert on the farther side of the river, so close, such an unreachable distance. One or two rode their horses down to the very edge of the water, but they gave up the thought and the whole troop turned back toward Wilsonville; even the horses were down-headed.

Back in the covert he found Bart lying with his head on his paws, his eyes closed, his sides swelling and closing till every rib seemed broken; yet now and then he opened one red eye to look at Satan. The stallion lay in almost exactly the same position, and the rush and rattle of his breathing was audible even in the noise of the Asper; Barry dropped prone and pressed his ear against the left side of the horse, just behind the shoulder. The fierce vibration fairly shook his head; he could *hear* the rush of the blood except when that deadly rattling of the breath came. When he rose to his knees the face of the master was serious, thoughtful.

"Satan!" he called, but the river must have drowned his voice. Only when he passed his fingers down the wet neck, one of Satan's ears pricked, and fell instantly back. It would not do to let him lie there in the cool mold by the water, for he knew that the greatest danger in overheating a horse is that it may cool too quickly afterward.

He stooped directly in front of Satan and swept up an arm in command; it brought only a flicker of the eyelid, the eyelid which dropped over a glazing eye.

"Up!" he commanded.

One ear again pricked; the head lifted barely clear of the ground; the forelegs stiffened with effort, trembled, and were still again.

"Bart!" shouted the master, "wake him up!"

The voice could not have carried to the wolf through the uproar of the waters, but the gesture, the expression brought home the order, and Black Bart came to his feet, staggering. Right against the nose of Satan he bared his great teeth and his snarl rattled. No living creature could hear that sound without starting, and the head of Satan raised high. Still before him Bart growled and under his elbow and his chest the hands of the master strained up. He swayed with a snort very like a human groan, struggled, the forelegs secured their purchase, and he came slowly to his feet. There he stood, braced and head low; a child might have caught him by the mane and toppled him upon his side, and already his hind legs were buckling.

"Get on!" cried Barry.

There was a lift of the head, a quivering of the tensed nostrils, but that was all. He seemed to be dying on his feet, when the master whistled. The sound cut through the rushing of the Asper as a ray of light probes a dark room, shrill, harsh, like the hissing of some incredible snake, and Satan went an uncertain step forward, reeled, almost fell; but the shoulder of the master was at his side lifting up, and the arm of the master was under his chest, raising. He tried another step; he went on among the trees with his forelegs sprawling and his head drooped as though he were trying to crop grass. Black Bart did his part to recall that flagging spirit. Sometimes it was his snarl that startled the black; sometimes he leaped, and his teeth clashed a hair's breadth from Satan's nose.

By degrees the congealing blood flowed freely again through Satan's body; he no longer staggered; and now he lifted a forepaw and struck vaguely at Bart as the wolf-dog leaped. Barry stepped away.

"Bart!" he called, and the shouting of the Asper was now so far away that he could be heard. "Come round here, old boy, and stop botherin' him. He's goin' to pull through."

He leaned against a willow, his face suddenly old and white with something more than exhaustion, and laughed in such an oddly pitched, cracked tone that the wolf-dog slunk to him on his belly and licked the dangling hand. He caught the scarred head of Bart and looked steadily down into the eyes of the wolf.

"It was a close call, Bart. There wasn't more than half an inch between Satan and——"

The black turned his head and whinnied feebly.

"Listen to him calllin' for help like a new-foaled colt," said the master, and went to Satan.

The head of the stallion rested on his shoulder as they went slowly on.

"To-night," said the master, "you get two pieces of pone without askin'." The cold nose of the jealous wolf-dog thrust against his left hand. "You too, Bart. You showed us the way."

The rattle had left the breathing of Satan, the stagger was gone from his walk; with each instant he grew perceptibly larger as they approached the border of the wood. It fell off to a scattering thicket with the Grizzly Peaks stepping swiftly up to the sky. This was their magic instant in all the day, when the sun, grown low in the west, with bulging sides, gave the mountains a yellow light. They swelled up larger with warm tints of gold rolling off into the blue of the canyons; at the foot of the nearest slope a thicket of quaking aspens was struck by a breeze and flashed all silver. Not many moments more, and all the peaks would be falling back into the evening.

It seemed that Satan saw this, for he raised his head from the shoulder of the master and stopped to look.

"Step on," commanded Barry.

The stallion shook himself violently as a dog that knocks water from his pelt, but he took no pace forward.

"Satan!"

The order made him sway forward, but he checked the movement.

"I ask you man to man, Bart," said the master in sudden anger, "was there ever a worse fool hoss than him? He won't budge till I get on his back."

The wolf-dog shoved his nose again into Barry's hand and growled. He seemed quite willing to go on alone with the master and leave Satan forgotten.

"All right," said Barry. "Satan, are you comin'?"

The horse whinnied, but would not move.

"Then stay here."

He turned his back and walked resolutely across the meadow, but slowly and more slowly, until a ringing neigh made him stop and turn. Satan had not stirred from his first halting place, but now his head was high and his ears pricked anxiously. He pawed the ground in his impatience.

"Look there, Bart," observed the master gloomily. "There's pride for you. He won't let on that he's too weak to carry me. Now I'd ought to let him stay there till he drops.

He whistled suddenly, the call sliding up, breaking, and rising again with a sharp appeal. Satan neighed again as it died away.

"If that won't bring him, nothin' will. Back we got to go. Bart, you jest take this to heart: It ain't any use tryin' to bring them to reason that ain't got any sense."

He went back and sprang lightly to the back of the horse and Satan staggered a little under the weight but once, as if to prove that his strength was more than equal to the task, he broke into a trot. A harsh order called him back to a walk, and so they started up into the Grizzly Peaks.

By dark, however, a few halts, a chance to crop grass for a moment here and there, a roll by the next creek and a short draught of water, restored a great part of the black's strength, and before the night was an hour old he was heading up through the hills at a long, swift trot.

Even then it was that dark, cold time just before dawn when they wound up the difficult pass toward the cave. The moon had gone down; a thin, high mist painted out the stars; and there were only varying degrees of blackness to show them the way, with peaks and ridges starting here and there out of the night, very suddenly. It was so dark, indeed, that sometimes Dan could not see where Bart skulked a little ahead, weaving among the boulders and picking the easiest way. But all three of them knew the course by instinct, and when they came to a more or less commanding rise of ground in the valley Dan checked the stallion and whistled.

Then he sat canting his head to one side to listen more intently. A rising wind brought about him something like an echo of the sound, but otherwise there was no answer.

"She ain't heard," muttered Dan to Bart, who came running back at the call, so familiar to him and to the horse. He whistled again, prolonging the call until it soared and trembled down the gulch, and this time when he stopped he sat for a long moment, waiting, until Black Bart whined at his side.

"She ain't learned to sleep light, yet," muttered Barry. "An' I s'pose she's plumb tired out waitin' for me. But if something's happened—Satan!"

That word sent the stallion leaping ahead at a racing gait, swerving among rocks which he could not see.

"They's nothin' wrong with her," whispered Barry to himself. "They *can't* be nothin' happened to her!"

He was in the cave, a moment later, standing in the center of the place with the torch high above his head; it flared and glimmered in the great eyes of Satan and the narrow eyes of Bart. At length he slipped down to a rock beside him while the torch, fallen from his hand, sputtered and whispered where it lay on the gravel.

"She's gone," he said to emptiness. "She's lef' me!"

Black Bart licked his limp hand but dared not even whine.

CHAPTER XXXVII

Ben Swann

Since the night when old Joe Cumberland died and Kate Cumberland rode off after her wild man, Ben Swann, the foreman of the Cumberland ranch, had lived in the big house. He would have been vastly more comfortable in the bunkhouse playing cards with the other hands, but Ben Swann felt vaguely that it was a shame for so much space in the ranch house to go to waste, and besides, Ben's natural dignity was at home in the place even if his mind grew lonely. It was Ben Swann, therefore, who ran down and flung open the door on which a heavy hand was beating. Outside stood two men, very tall, taller than himself, and one of them a giant. They had about them a strong scent of horses.

"Get a light" said one of these. "Run for it. Get a light. Start a fire, and be damned quick about it!"

"And who the hell might you gents be?" queried Ben Swann, leaning against the side of the doorway to dicker.

"Throw that fool on his head," said one of the strangers, "and go on in, Lee!"

"Stand aside," said the other, and swept the door knob out of Ben's grip, flattening Ben himself against the wall. While he struggled there, gasping, a man and a woman slipped past him.

"Tell him who we are," said the woman's voice. "We'll go to the living-room, Buck, and start a fire."

The strangers apparently knew their way even in the dark, for presently he heard the scraping of wood on the hearth in the living-room. It bewildered Ben Swann. It was dream-like, this sudden invasion.

"Now, who the devil are you?"

A match was scratched and held under his very nose, until Ben shrank back for fear that his splendid mustaches might ignite. He found himself confronted by one of the largest men he had ever seen, a leonine face, vaguely familiar.

"You Lee Haines!" he gasped. "What are you doin' here?"

"You're Swann, the foreman, aren't you?" said Haines. "Well, come out of your dream, man. The owner of the ranch is in the living-room."

"Joe Cumberland's dead," stammered Ben Swann.

"Kate Cumberland."

"Her! And—Barry—the Killing at Alder——"

"Shut up!" ordered Haines, and his face grew ugly. "Don't let that chatter get to Kate's ears. Barry ain't with her. Only his kid. Now stir about."

After the first surprise was over, Ben Swann did very well. He found the fire already started in the living-room and on the rug before the hearth a yellow-haired little girl wrapped in a tawny hide. She was sound asleep, worn out by the long ride, and she seemed to Ben Swann a very pretty picture. Surely there could be in her little of the father of whom he had heard so much—of whom the story of the Killing at Alder was lately told. He took in that picture at a glance and then went to rustle food; afterward he went down to sleep in the bunkhouse and at breakfast he recounted the events of the night with a relish. Not one of the men had been more than three years on the place, and therefore their minds were clean slates on which Swann could write his own impressions.

"Appearances is deceivin'," concluded the foreman. "Look at Mrs. Dan Barry. They tell you around these parts that she's pretty, but they don't tell you how *damned* fine lookin' she is. She's got a soft look and you'd never pick her for the sort that would run clean off with a gent like Barry. Barry himself wasn't so bad for looks, but they'll tell you in Elkhead how bad he is in action, and maybe they's some widders in Alder that could put in a word. Take even the kid. She looks no more'n a baby, but what d'you know is inside of her?

"Speakin' personal, gents, I don't put no kind of trust

in that houseful yonder. Here they come in the middle of the night like there was a posse after 'em. They climb that house and sit down and eat like they'd ridden all day. Maybe they had. Even while they was eatin' they didn't seem none too happy.

"That loose shutter upstairs come around in the wind with a bang and Buck Daniels comes out of his chair as fast as powder could blow him. He didn't say nothin'. Just sat down lookin' kind of sick, and the other two was the same way. When they talked, they'd bust off in the middle of a word and let their eyes go trailin' into some corner of the room that was plumb full of shadow. Then Lee Haines gets up and walks up and down.

" 'Swann,' says he, 'how many good men have you got on the place?'

" 'Why,' says I, 'they're all good!'

" 'Huh,' says Haines, and he puts a hand on my shoulder, 'just how good are they, Swann?' "

"I seen what he wanted. He wanted to know how many scrappy gents was punchin' cows here; maybe them three up there figures that they might need help. From what? What was they runnin' away from?"

"Hey!" broke in one of the cowpunchers, pointing with a dramatic fork through the window.

It was a bright spot of gold that disappeared over the top of the nearest hill; then it came into view again the whole body of a yellow-haired child, clothed in a wisp of white, and running steadily toward the north.

"The kid!" gasped the foreman. "Boys, grab her. No, you'd bust her; I know how to handle her!"

He was gone through the door with gigantic leaps and shot over the crest of the low hill. Then those in the cookhouse heard a small, tingling scream; after it, came silence, and the tall foreman striding across the hill with the child high in his arms. He came panting through the door and stood her up on the end of the table, a small and fearless creature. She wore on her feet the little moccasins which Dan himself had fashioned for her, but the tawny hide was not on her—perhaps her mother had thrown the garment away. The moccasins and the white nightgown were the sum and substance of her apparel, and the cowpunchers stood up around the table to admire her spunk.

"Darned near spat pizen," observed Ben Swann, "when I hung into her—tried to bite me, but the minute I got her in my hands she quit strugglin' as reasonable as a grown-up, by God!"

"Shut up, Ben. Don't you know no better'n to cuss in front of a kid?"

The great dark eyes of Joan went somberly from face to face. If she was afraid, she disguised it well, but now and then, like a wild thing which sees that escape is impossible, she looked through the window and out over the open country beyond.

"Where was you headed for, honey?" queried Ben Swann.

The child considered him bravely for a time before she replied.

"Over there."

"Over there? Now what might she mean by that? Headed for Elkhead—in a nightgown? Any place I could take you, kid?"

If she did not altogether trust Ben Swann, at least she preferred him to the other unshaven, work-thinned faces which leered at her around the table.

"Daddy Dan," she said softly. "Joan wants to go to Daddy Dan."

"Daddy Dan—Dan Barry," translated Ben Swann, and he drew a bit away from her. "Boys, that man-killin' devil must be around here; and that's what them up at the house was runnin' from—Barry!"

It scattered the others to the windows, to the door.

"What d'you see?"

"Nothin'."

"Swann, if Barry is comin' to these parts, I'm goin' to pack my war-bag."

"Me too, Ben. Them that get ten thousand'll earn it. *I* heard about the Killin' at Alder."

"Listen to me, gents," observed Ben Swann. "If Barry is comin' here we ain't none of us goin' to stay; but don't start jumpin' out from under till I get the straight of it. I'm goin' to take the kid up to the house right now and find out."

So he wrapped up Joan in an old blanket, for she was shivering in the cold of the early morning, and carried her up to the ranchhouse. The alarm had already been given. He saw Buck Daniels gallop toward the front of the place leading two saddled horses; he saw Haines and Kate run down the steps to meet them, and then they caught sight of the foreman coming with Joan on his shoulder.

The joy of that meeting, it seemed to Ben Swann, was decidedly one-sided. Kate ran to Joan with a little wailing cry of happiness and gathered her close, but neither big Lee Haines nor ugly Buck Daniels seemed overcome with happiness at the regaining of Joan, and the child herself merely endured the caresses of her mother. Ben Swann made them a speech.

He told them that anybody with half an eye could tell they were bothered by something, that they acted as if they were running away. Now, running in itself was perfectly all right and quite in order when it was impossible to outface or outbluff a danger. He himself, Ben Swann, believed in such tactics. He wasn't a soldier; he was a cowpuncher. So were the rest of the boys out yonder, and though they'd stay by their work in ordinary times, and they'd face ordinary trouble, they were not minded to abide the coming of Dan Barry.

"So," concluded Swann, "I want to ask you straight. Is him they call Whistlin' Dan comin' this way? Are you runnin' from him? And did you steal the kid from him?"

Lee Haines took upon his competent shoulders the duty of answering.

"You look like a sensible man, Swann," he said severely. "I'm surprised at you. In the first place, two men don't run away from one."

A fleeting smile appeared and disappeared on the lips of Ben Swann. Haines hastily went on: "As for stealing the baby from Dan Barry, good heavens, man, don't you think a mother has a right to her own child? Now go back to that scared bunch and tell them that Dan Barry is back in the Grizzly Peaks."

For several reasons this did not completely satisfy the

216

foreman, but he postponed his decision. Lee Haines spoke like one in the habit of giving orders, and Swann walked slowly back to the cookhouse.

CHAPTER XXXVIII

The New Alliance

"And so," said Lee Haines, when he joined Buck Daniels in the living-room, "there goes our reinforcements. That whole crew will scatter like dead leaves when Barry breezes in. It looks to me——"

"Shut up!" cut in Daniels. "Shut up!"

His dark, homely face turned to the larger man with a singular expression of awe. He whispered: "D'you hear? She's in the next room whippin' Joan for runnin' away, and never a yap out of the kid!"

He held up a lean finger for caution and then Haines heard the sound of the willow switch. It stopped.

"If you run away again," warned Kate, her voice pitched high and trembling, "munner will whip harder, and put you in a dark place for a long, long time."

Still there was not a sound of the child's voice, not even the pulse of stifled weeping. Presently the door opened and Kate stood there.

"Go out in the kitchen and tell Li to give you breakfast. Naughty girls can't eat with munner."

Through the door came Joan, her little round face perfectly white, perfectly expressionless. She did not cringe, passing her mother; she walked steadily across the room, rose on tip-toe to open the kitchen door, and disappeared through it. Kate dropped into a chair, shaking.

"Out!" whispered Buck to Lee Haines. "Beat it. I got to talk alone." And as soon as Haines obeyed, Buck sat down close to the girl. She was twisting and untangling her fingers in a dumb agony.

"What has he done to her, Buck? What has he done?"

It was a maxim with Buck that talk is to a woman what

swearing is to man; it is a safety valve, and therefore he waited in silence until the first rush of her grief had passed.

"She only looked at me when I whipped her. My heart turned in me. She didn't cry; she wasn't even angry. She just stood there—my baby!—and looked at me!"

She threw herself back in the chair with her eyes closed, and he saw where the trouble had marked her face. He wanted to lean over and take her in his arms.

"I'm going mad, Buck. I can't stand it. How could he have changed her to this?"

"Listen to me, Kate. Joan ain't been changed. She's only showin' what she is."

The mother stared wildly at him.

"Don't look like I was a murderer. God knows I'm sorry, Kate, but if they's Dan's blood in your little girl it ain't my fault. It ain't anything he's taught her. It's just that bein' alone with him has brought out what she really is."

"I won't believe you, Buck. I don't dare listen to you!"

"You got to listen, Kate, because you know I'm right. D'you think that any kind of teachin' could make her learn how to stand and keep from cryin' when she was whipped?"

"I know."

She spoke softly, as if some terrible power might overhear them talk, and Buck lowered his voice in turn.

"She's wild, Kate, I knew it when I seen the way she handled Bart. She's wild!"

"Then I'll have her tame again."

"You tried that once and failed."

"Dan was a man when I tried, and his nature was formed. Joan is only a baby—my baby. She's half mine. She has my hair and my eyes."

"I don't care what the color of her eyes is, I know what's behind them., Look at 'em, and then tell me who she takes after."

"Buck, why do you talk like this? What do you want me to do?"

"A hard thing. Send Joan back to Dan."

"Never!"

"He'll never give her up, I tell you."

"Oh, God help me. What shall I do? I'll keep her! I'll make her tame."

"But you'll never keep her that way. Think of Dan. Think of the yaller in his eyes, Kate."

"Until I die," she said with sudden quiet, "I'll fight to keep her."

And he answered with equal solemnity: "Until Dan dies he'll fight to have her. And he's never been beat yet."

Through a breathing space he stared at her and she at him, and the eyes of Buck Daniels were the first to turn. Everything that was womanly and gentle had died from her face, and in its stead was something which made Buck rise and wander from the room.

He found Lee Haines and told him briefly all that had passed. The great battle, they decided, had begun between Kate and Barry for the sake of the child, and that battle would go on until one of them was dead or the prize for which they struggled lost. Barry would come on the trail and find them at the ranch, and then he would strike for Joan. And they had no help for the struggle against him. The cowpunchers would scatter at the first sign of Barry, at the first shrill of his ill-omened whistling. They might ride for Elkhead and raise a posse from among the citizens, but it would take two days to do that and gather a number of effective fighters for the crisis, and in the meantime the chances were large that Barry would strike the ranch while the messenger was away. There was really nothing to do but sit patiently and wait. They were both brave men, very; and they were both not unpracticed fighters; but they began to wait for the coming of Barry as the prisoner waits for the day of his execution.

It spoke well for the quality of their nerves that they would not speak to Kate of the time to come; they sat back like spectators at a play and watched the maneuvers of the mother to win back Joan.

There was not an idle moment from breakfast to dark. They went out to gather wildflowers on the western hill from the house; they sat on the veranda where Kate told Joan stories of the ranch and pointed out the distant mountains which were its boundaries, and explained that all between them would one day be her own land; that the men who rode yonder were doing her work; that the cattle who ranged the hills were marked with her brand. She said it all in small words so that Joan could understand, but as far as Buck and Lee could make out, there was never a flicker of intelligence or interest in the eyes of the child.

It was a hard battle every hour, and after supper Kate sat in a big chair by the fire with her eyes half closed, admitting defeat, perhaps. For Joan was curled up on the couch at the farthest, dimmest end of the room, and with her chin propped in both small hands she stared in silence through the window and over the darkening hills. Buck and Lee were there, never speaking, but now and then their eyes sought each other with a vague hope. For Kate might see that her task was impossible, send Joan back, and that would free them of the danger.

But where Kate left off, chance took up the battle and turned the scales. Old Li, the Chinese cook, had not seen Kate for six long years, and now he celebrated the return by hanging about her on a thousand pretexts. It was just after he had brought in some delicacy from the kitchen, leaving the door a little ajar, when a small ball of gray fur nosed its way through the aperture and came straight for the glare of the fire on the hearth. It was a small shepherd puppy, and having observed the faces of the men with bright unafraid eyes, it went wobbling on to the very hearth, sniffling. Even at that age it knew enough to keep away from the bright coals of wood, but how could it know that the dark, cold-looking andirons had been heated to the danger point by the fire? It thrust out a tentative nose, touched the iron, and then its shrill yelp of pain went startlingly through the room. It pulled the three grown-ups out of their thoughts; it brought Joan scampering across the room with a little happy cry.

The puppy would have escaped if it could, for it had in mind the dark, warm, familiar corner in Li's kitchen where no harm ever came near, but the agile hands of Joan caught him; he was swept into her arms. That little wail of helpless pain, the soft fluff of fur against her cheek, wiped all other things from Joan's mind. Out the window and across the gloomy hills she had been staring at the picture of the cave, and bright-eyed Satan, and the shadowy form of Bart, and the swift, gentle hand of Daddy Dan; but the cry of the puppy blotted the picture out. She was no longer lonely, having this small, soft body to protect. There sat her mother, leaning a little toward her with a glance at once misted and bright, and she forgot forthwith all the agency of Kate in carrying her away from that cave of delight.

"Look, munner! He's burned his nose!"

The puppy was licking the injured nose industriously and whimpering the while. And Joan heard no answer from her mother except an inarticulate little sound somewhere deep in Kate's throat. Over her child mind, vaguely, like all baby memories, moved a recollection of the same sound, coming deeply from the throat of the mother and marvelously soothing, reassuring. It moved a fiber of trust and sympathy in Joan, an emotion as real as the sound of music, and with the puppy held idly in her arms for a moment, she looked curiously into Kate's face. On her own, a faint smile began in the eyes and spread to the lips.

"Poor little puppy, munner," said Joan.

The hands of Kate trembled with desire to bring Joan closer to her, but very wisely she merely stroked the cringing head of the dog.

"Poor little puppy," she echoed.

CHAPTER XXXIX

Victory

The entrance of the puppy, to liken small things to great, was the coming of Blücher in Kate's life, for the battle turned, and all in five minutes she had gone from defeat to victory. She sat by the fire with Joan sleeping in her arms, and the puppy in turn in the arms of Joan. It was such a foolish trick of chance that had given her all this, she was almost inclined to laugh, but something of tragedy in the faces of Buck and Lee Haines made her thoroughly serious. And she readily saw the truth. For after all a child's brain is a small affair; it holds so much and no more. One instant the longing for Dan was all that Joan could think of; the next she had no room for anything more than the burned nose of the puppy. If there were other phases to this matter—such as Buck Daniels had pointed out—fear that in some future crisis the blood of the father might show in the child, Kate pushed such thoughts away. She was too full of the present happiness.

Now, while she sat there in the firelight, she sang softly into the dreams of Joan, and watched the smile of sleep grow and wane faintly on the lips of the child as the rhythm of her singing lifted and fell. One half of her mind was empty, that part where Dan should have been, and a dozen times she checked an impulse to turn to him in the place where he should be sitting and invite him with a smile to share her happiness. When her eyes moved they only fell on the gaunt, intent face of Buck or the leonine head of Haines. Whistling Dan was gone and if he ever came again her fear of him, her fear for Joan, would be greater than her love. Yet Dan being gone so finally, she knew that she would never be truly happy again. Her spring of life was ended, but even now she was grateful for the full richness of those six years with Dan; and if she turned from him now it was only because a mighty instinct commanded her and a voice without words drove her: Joan must go on to a normal, womanly happiness. Dan Barry lived from day to day, glutting himself with a ride in the wind, or the whistle of a far-off bird, or the wail of a mountain-lion through the night. Each instant was to him complete, but the eye of Kate looked far away and saw the night when this daughter of hers should sit holding an infant by such a fire, and her heart was both empty and full.

It was no wonder, then, that she heard the first sound long before either Haines or Buck Daniels, for her mind was on guard against dangers which might threaten her baby. It was a faint slipping, scratching noise on the veranda; then a breathing at the front door. Kate turned, and the men followed the terror of her eyes in time to see the door fall open, and a broad paw appear in the interval. The snaky head of Black Bart thrust into the room.

Without a word, Daniels drew his gun.

"Wait!" commanded Kate. Joan awoke with a start at the sharpness of this voice. "Don't shoot, Buck. See that bit of paper under his throat. He's bringing a message."

"Bart!" cried Joan, slipping to the floor from her mother's lap, but when she ran toward the wolf-dog, that tremendous snarl of warning stopped her short. Bart slunk toward Kate.

"Look out, Kate!" cried Haines. "That black devil means murder."

"Don't move, or he'll go at your throat," she answered. "There's no danger to me. He's been ordered to go to me and he won't let even Joan touch him. See!"

He had glided past the amazed, outstretched arms of Joan and went straight to Kate and stopped beside her, obviously expectant. She reached for the slip of folded paper, and as her hand approached he crouched a little, growling; but it was only to caution her, apparently, and though he distrusted the hand, he allowed it to unfasten the missive.

She untwisted the note, she read aloud: "Kate send Joan back to me or I come for her. Send her with Bart."

It seemed as though the wolf-dog understood the written words, for now he moved toward Joan and she, with a cry, dropped the squealing puppy and caught the great head of Bart in her arms. The puppy wailed, sitting down on his haunches, and quivering with grief.

"Daddy Dan wants me," explained Joan with bright eyes. "He's sent for me. Go quick, Bart!"

The big animal lay down to facilitate her mounting.

"Joan!" called Kate. The child hesitated and turned toward her. Her mother had taken up that light revolver which Dan had taught her to use so well, and now, as she leveled it at the wolf-dog, Bart laid his fangs bare in silent hate. The weapons of Buck and Lee Haines were ready, and now Bart raised himself a little and commenced to drag gradually forward to leaping distance.

"Drop your gun, Kate," cautioned Buck. "For God's sake drop your gun. Even if you hit him with a bullet, he'll be at your throat. Unless you kill him with the first shot he'll have you. Drop your gun and then he'll go at us."

But Joan knew perfectly well what those gleaming bits of steel meant. She had seen Daddy Dan shoot and kill, and now she ran screaming between Bart and danger.

"Munner!" she cried. "You bad, bad men. I won't let you hurt Bart."

"They won't hurt you, Bart," explained Joan, turning much mollified to the great wolf-dog. "They're just playin'. Now we'll go."

And she started toward the door, with Bart slinking in front and keeping a watchful lookout from a corner of his eye.

"Are you going to leave the poor little puppy, Joan?" said the mother, keeping her voice steady, for all the force of the two men could not help her now. It rested with her wit.

"I'll take him with me," answered Joan, and caught up the howling puppy from the floor. His wails died out against her breast.

"But you mustn't do that honey. He'd die in this cold night wind long before you got there."

"Oh!" sighed Joan, and considered her mother with great eyes. Black Bart turned and uneasily tugged at her dress.

"Will you take good care of him, munner? Till I come back?"

"But I don't know how to take care of him, dear. If you go he'll cry and cry and cry until he dies."

Joan sighed.

"See how quiet he is when you hold him, Joan!"

"Oh," muttered Joan again. The distress of the problem made her wrinkle her forehead. She turned to Kate for help.

"Munner, what'll I do?"

"You'd best stay here until the puppy is strong enough to go with you."

She kept her voice well under control; it would not do to show the slightest emotion, and now she sat down and half turned away from the child. With her eyes she flashed a signal at the two troubled men and they followed her lead. Their center of vision was now upon the fire. It left Joan, to all appearances quite out of notice.

"Oh, that'll be a long, long time, munner."

"Only a little while, Joan."

"But Daddy Dan'll be lonesome up there."

"He has Satan and Bart to keep him company."

"Don't you think he wants Joan, munner?"

"Not as much as the poor little puppy wants you, Joan."

She added, with just the slightest tremor: "You decide for yourself, Joan. Go if you think it is best."

"Bart, what'll Joan do?" queried the child, turning in dismay toward the wolf-dog, but as soon as he saw the puppy in her arms, he greeted her with a murderous snarl.

"You see," suggested her mother, "that Black Bart would eat up the poor little puppy if you went now with him."

At this alarming thought, Joan shrank away from Bart

and when he followed her, anxiously, she cried: "Go away! Bad dog! Bad Bart!"

He caught the edge of her dress and drew back toward the door, and this threw Joan into a sudden panic. She struck Bart across his wrinkled forehead.

"Go away!" he slunk back, snarling at the puppy.

"Go back to Daddy Dan." Then, as he pricked his ears, still growling like distant thunder: "Go tell Daddy Dan that Joan has to stay here a while. Munner, how long?"

"Maybe a week, dear."

"A whole week?" she cried, dismayed.

"Perhaps only one or two or three days," said Kate.

Some of her tenseness was leaving as she saw victory once more inclining to her standards.

"One, two, five days," counted Joan, "and then come for me again. Tell Daddy Dan that, Bart."

His eyes left her and wandered around the room, lingering for a vicious instant on the face of each, then he backed toward the door.

"He's clear of Joan now, Kate," whispered Buck. "Let me shoot!"

"No, no! Don't even look at him."

Then, with a scratching of sudden claws, Bart whirled at the door and was gone like a bolt down the hall. Afterwards for a time there was no sound in the room except the murmurings of Joan to her puppy, and then they heard that most mournful of sounds on the mountain-desert, the long howl of a wolf which has missed its kill, and hunts hungry on a new trail.

CHAPTER XL

The Failure

When Black Bart returned without Joan, without even
a note of answer about his neck, the master made ready
to take by force. First he went over his new outfit of
saddle and guns, looking to every strap of the former,
and the latter, revolvers and rifle, he weighed and balanced with a meditative look, as if he were memo-
rizing their qualities against a time of need. With Satan
saddled and Bart on guard at the mouth of the cave, he
gathered up all the accumulation of odds and ends, pro-
visions, skins, and made a stirring bonfire in the middle
of the gravel floor. It was like burning his bridges before
starting out to the battle; he turned his back to the cave
and started on his journey.

He had to travel in a loose semicircle, for there were
two points which he must reach on the ride, the town
of Alder, where lived the seventh man who must die for
Grey Molly, and the Cumberland ranch, last of all, where
he would take Joan. Very early after his start he reached
the plateau where he had lived all those years with Kate,
and he found it already sinking back to ruin, with nothing
in the corrals, and the front door swinging to and fro
idly in the wind, just as Joan had often played with it.
Inside, he knew, the rooms were empty; a current of air
down the chimney had scattered the ashes from the hearth
all about the living room. Here must be a chair over-
turned, and there the sand had drifted through the open
door. All this he saw clearly enough with his mind's eye,
and urged Satan forward. For a chill like the falling of
sudden night had swept over him, and he shrugged his
shoulders with relief when he swept past the house. Yet

when he came to the long down-slope which pitched into the valley so far below him, he called Satan to a halt again, and swung to look at the house. He could hear the clatter of the front door as it swung; it seemed to be waving a farewell to him.

It was all the work of a moment, to ride back, gather a quantity of paper and readily inflammable. materials, soak them in oil, and scratch a match. The flames swept up the sides of the logs and caught on the ceiling first of all, and Dan Barry stood in the center of the room until the terrified whining of Black Bart and the teeth of the wolf-dog at his trousers made him turn and leave the house. Outside, he found Satan trembling between two temptations, the first to run as far and as fast as he could from that most terrible thing—fire; and the second to gallop straight into the blaze. The voice of the master, a touch quieted him, and Black Bart lay down at the feet of the master and looked up into his face.

By this time the fire had licked away a passage through the roof and through this it sent up a yellow hand that flicked up and down like a signal, or a beckoning, and then shot up a tall, steady, growing, roaring column of red. No man could say what went through the mind of Dan Barry as he stood there watching the house of his building burn, but now he turned and threw his arms over the neck and back of Satan, and dropped his forehead against the withers of the black. It troubled the stallion. He turned his head, and nosed the shoulder of the master gently, and Black Bart, in an agony of anxiety, reared up beside Dan and brought his head almost up to the head of the man; there he whined pleadingly for never before had he seen the master hide his face.

A deep, short report made the master stand away from Satan. The fire had reached a small stock of powder, and the shock of the explosion was followed by a great crashing and rending as an inner wall went down. That fall washed a solid mass of yellow flame across the front door, but the fire fell back, and then Dan saw the doll which he himself had made for Joan; it had been thrown by the smashing of the wall squarely in front of the door, and now the fire reached after it—long arms across the floor. It was an odd contrivance, singularly made of carved wood and with arms and legs fastened on by means of bits of strong sinew, and Joan prized it above all the rosy faced dolls which Kate had bought for her. For an instant Dan stood watching the progress of the fire, then he leaped through the door, swerved back as an arm of fire shot out at him, ran forward again, caught up the doll and was outside rubbing away the singed portions of brows and lashes.

He did not wait until the house was consumed, but when the flames stood towering above the roof, shaking out to one side with a roar when the wind struck them, he mounted Satan once more, and made for the valley.

He wanted to reach Alder at dark, and he gauged the time of his ride so accurately that when he pulled out of the mouth of Murphy's Pass, the last light of the day was still on the mountains and in the pass, but it was already dark in the village, and a score of lights twinkled up at him like eyes.

He left Satan and Bart well outside the town, for even in the dark they might easily be recognized, and then walked straight down the street of Alder. It was a bold thing to do, but he knew that the first thing which is seen and suspected is the skulker who approaches from covert to covert. They knew he had ridden into Alder before in the middle of the night and they might suspect the danger of such another attack, but they surely would not have fear of a solitary pedestrian unless a telltale light were thrown upon his face.

He passed Captain Lorrimer's saloon. Even in this short interval it had fallen into ill-repute after the killing at Alder. And a shanty farther down the street now did the liquor business of the town; Captain Lorrimer's was closed, and the window nailed across with slats. He went on. Partly by instinct, and partly because it was aflame with lights, he moved straight to the house at which he had learned tidings of three men he sought on his last visit to Alder. Now there were more lights showing from the windows of that place than there were in all the rest of Alder; at the hitching racks in front, horses stood tethered in long double rows, and a noise of voices rolled out and up and down the street. Undoubtedly, there was a festival there, and all Alder would turn out to such an affair. All Alder, including Vic Gregg, the seventh man. A group came down the street for the widow's house; they were laughing and shouting, and they carried lanterns; away from them Barry slipped like a ghost and stood in the shadow of the house.

There might be other such crowds, and they were dangerous to Barry so now he hunted for a means of breaking into the house of the widow unseen. The windows, as he went down the side of the building, he noted to be high, but not too high to be reached by a skillful, noiseless climber. In the back of the house he saw the kitchen door, illumined indeed, but the room, as far as he could see, empty.

Then very suddenly a wave of silence began somewhere in the side of the house and swept across it, dying to a murmur at the edges. Barry waited for no more maneuvers, but walked boldly up the back stairs and entered the house, hat in hand.

The moment he passed the door he was alert, balanced. He could have swung to either side, or whirled and shot behind him with the precision of a leisurely marksman, and as he walked he smiled, happily with his head held high. He seemed so young, then, that one would have said he had just come in gaily from some game with the other youths of Alder.

Out of the kitchen he passed into the hall, and there he understood the meaning of the silence, for both the doors to the front room were open, and through the doors he heard a single voice, deep and solemn, and through the doors he saw the crowd standing motionless. Their heads did not stir,—heads on which the hair was plastered smoothly down—and when some one raised a hand to touch an itching ear, or nose, he moved his arm with such caution that it seemed he feared to set a magazine of powder on fire. All their backs were towards Barry, where he stood in the hall, and as he glided toward them, he heard the deep voice stop, and then the trembling voice of a girl speak in reply.

231

At the first entrance he paused, for the whole scene unrolled before him. It was a wedding. Just in front of him, on chairs and even on benches, sat the majority of adult Alder,—facing these stood the wedding pair with the minister just in front of them. He could see the girl to one side of the minister's back, and she was very pretty, very femininely appealing, now, in a dress which was a cloudy effect of white; but Barry gave her only one sharp glance. His attention was for the men of the crowd. And although there were only backs of heads, and side glimpses of faces he hunted swiftly for Vic Gregg.

But Gregg was not there. He surveyed the assembly twice, incredulous, for surely the tall man should be here, but when he was on the very point of turning on his heel and slinking down the hall to pursue his hunt in other quarters, the voice of the minister stopped, and the deep tone of Vic himself rolled through the room.

It startled Barry like a voice out of the sky; he stared about, bewildered, and then as the minister shifted his position a little he saw that it was Gregg being married. And at the same moment, the eyes of Vic lifted, wandered, fell upon the face which stood there framed in the dark of the doorway. Dan saw the flush die out, saw the narrow, single-purposed face of Gregg turn white, saw his eyes widen, and his own hand closed on his gun. Another instant; the minister turned his head, seemed to be waiting, and then Gregg spoke in answer: "I will!"

A thousand pictures rushed through the mind of Barry, and he remembered first and last the wounded man on the gray horse who he had saved, and the long hard ride carrying that limp body to the cabin in the mountains. The man would fight. By the motion of Gregg's hand, Dan knew that he had gone even to his wedding armed. He had only to show his own gun to bring on the crisis, and in the meantime the eyes of Vic held steadily upon him past the shoulder of the minister, without fear, desperately. In spite of himself Dan's hand could not move his gun. In spite of himself he looked to the confused happy face of the girl. And he felt as he had felt when he set fire to his house up there in the hills. The wavering lasted only a

232

moment longer; then he turned and slipped noiselessly down the hall, and the seventh man who should have died for Grey Molly was still alive.

CHAPTER XLI

The Wild Geese

Twenty-four hours from Alder to Elkhead, and beyond Elkhead to the Cumberland ranch, is long riding and hard riding, but not far after dark on the following night, Joan lifted her head, where she played with the puppy on the hearth, and listened. There was no sound audible to the others in the living room; they did not even mark the manner in which she sat up, and then rose to her feet. But when she whispered "Daddy Dan!" it brought each of the three out of his chair. Still they heard nothing, and Buck and Lee Haines would have retaken their chairs had not Kate gone to the window and thrown it wide. Then they caught it, very far off, very thin and small, a delicate thread of music, an eerie whistling. Without a word, she closed the window, crossed the room and from the table she took up a cartridge belt from which hung the holster with the revolver which Whistling Dan taught her to use so well. She buckled it about her. Lee Haines and Daniels, without a word, imitated her actions. Their guns were already on—every moment since they reached the ranch they had gone armed—but now they looked to them, and tried the actions a few times before they thrust them back into the holsters.

It was odd to watch them. They were like the last remnant of a garrison, outworn with fighting, which prepares in grim quiet for the final stand.

The whistling rose a little in volume now. It was a happy sound, without a recognizable tune, but a gay, wild improvisation as if a violinist, drunk, was remembering snatches of masterpieces, throwing out lovely fragments here and there and filling the intervals out of his own excited fancy. Joan ran to the window, forgetful of the puppy, and kneeled there in the chair, looking out. The whistling stopped as Kate drew down the curtain to cut out Joan's view. It was far too dark for the child to see out, but she often would sit like this, looking into the dark.

The whistling began again as Joan turned silently on her mother, uncomplaining, but with a singular glint in her eyes, a sort of flickering, inward light that came out by glances and starts. Now the sound of the rider blew closer and closer. Kate gestured the men to their positions, one for each of the two inner doors while she herself took the outer one. There was not a trace of color in her face, but otherwise she was as calm as a stone, and from her an atmosphere pervaded the room, so that the men also stood quietly at their posts, without a word, without a sign to each other. They had their unspoken order from Kate. She would resist to the death and she expected the same from them. They were prepared.

Still that crescendo of the whistling continued; it seemed as if it would never reach them; it grew loud as a bird singing in that very room, and still it continued to swell, increase—then suddenly went out. As if it were the signal for which she had been waiting all these heartbreaking moments, Kate opened the front door, ran quickly down the hall, and stood an instant later on the path in front of the house. She had locked the doors as she went through, and now she heard one of the men rattling the lock to follow her. The rattling ceased. Evidently they decided that they would hold the fort as they were.

Her heel hardly sank in the sand when she saw him. He came out of the night like a black shadow among shadows, with the speed of the wind to carry him. A light creak of leather as he halted, a glimmer of star light on Satan as he wheeled, a clink of steel, and then Dan was coming up the path.

She knew him perfectly even before she could make out the details of the form; she knew him by the light, swift, almost noiseless step, like the padding footfall of a great cat—a sense of weight without sound. Another form skulked behind him—Black Bart.

235

He was close, very close, before he stopped, or seemed to see her, though she felt that he must have been aware of her since he first rode up. He was so close, indeed, that the starlight—the brim of his hat standing up somewhat from the swift riding—showed his face quite clearly to her. It was boyish, almost in its extreme youth, and so thinly molded, and his frame so lightly made, that he seemed one risen from a wasting bed of sickness. The wind fluttered his shirt and she wondered, as she had wondered so often before, where he gained that incredible strength in so meager a body. In all her life she had never loved him as she loved him now. But her mind was as fixed as a star.

"You can't have her, Dan. You can't have her! Don't you see how terrible a thing you'd make her? She's my blood, my pain, my love, and you want to take her up yonder to the mountains and the loneliness—I'll die to keep her!"

Now the moon, which had been buried in a drift of clouds, broke through them, and seemed in an instant to slide a vast distance towards the earth, a crooked half moon with its edges eaten by the mist. Under this light she could see him more clearly, and she became aware of the thing she dreaded, the faint smile which barely touched at the corners of his mouth; and in his eyes a swirl of yellow light, half guessed at, half real. All her strength poured out of her. She felt her knees buckle, felt the fingers about the light revolver butt relax, felt every nerve grow slack. She was helpless, and it was not fear of the man, but of something which stalked behind him, inhuman, irresistible; not the wolf-dog, but something more than Satan, and Bart, and Whistling Dan, something of which they were only a part.

He began to whistle, thoughtfully, like one who considers a plan of action and yet hesitates to begin. She felt his eyes run over her, as if judging how he should put her most gently to one side; then from the house, very lightly, hardly more than an echo of Dan's whistling, came an answer—the very same refrain. Joan was calling to him.

At that he stepped forward, but the thing which stirred

him, had hardened the mind of Kate. The weakness passed in a flash. It was Joan, and for Joan!

"Not a step!" she whispered, and jerked out her gun. "Not a step!"

He stood with one hand trailing carelessly from his hip, and at the gleam of her steel his other hand dropped to a holster, fumbled there, and came away empty; he could not touch her, not with the weight of a finger. That thoughtful whistle came again; once more the answering whistle drifted out from the house; and he moved forward another pace.

She had chosen her mark carefully, the upper corner of the seam of the pocket upon his shirt, and before his foot struck the ground she fired. For an instant she felt that she missed the mark, for he stood perfectly upright, but then she saw that the yellow was gone from his eyes. They were empty of everything except a great wonder. He wavered to his knees, and then sank down with his arms around Black Bart. He seemed, indeed to crumple away into the night. Then she heard a shouting and trampling in the house, and a breaking open of the doors, and she knew that she had killed Whistling Dan. She would have gone to him, but the snarl of Bart drove her back. Then she saw Satan galloping up the path and come to a sliding halt where he stood with his delicate nose close to the face of the master. There was no struggle with death, only a sigh like a motion of wind in far off trees, and then, softly, easily Black Bart extricated himself from the master, and moved away down the path, all wolf, all wild. Behind him, Satan whirled with a snort, and they rushed away into the night each in an opposite direction. The long companionship of the three was ended, and the seventh man was dead for Grey Molly.

Lee Haines and Buck Daniels were around her now. She heard nothing distinctly, only a great, vague clamor of voices while she kneeled and turned the body of Barry on its back. It was marvelously light; she could almost have picked it up in her arms, she felt. She folded the hands across his breast, and the limp fingers were delicate as the fingers of a sick child. Buck Daniels lay prone by the dead man weeping aloud; and Lee Haines stood with his face buried in his hands; but there was no tear on the face of Kate.

As she closed the eyes, the empty, hollow eyes, she heard a distant calling, a hoarse and dissonant chiming. She looked up and saw a wedge of wild geese flying low across the moon.